MW00587379

Death on the Lonely Llano Estacado

Death on the Lonely Llano Estacado

The Assassination of J. W. Jarrott, a Forgotten Hero

Bill Neal

Foreword by Chuck Lanehart

Number 17 in the A.C. Greene Series

Denton, Texas

Printed in the United States of America.

10 9 8 7 6 5 4 3 2 1

Permissions:
University of North Texas Press
1155 Union Circle #311336
Denton, TX 76203-5017

The paper used in this book meets the minimum requirements of the American National Standard for Permanence of Paper for Printed Library Materials, z39.48.1984. Binding materials have been chosen for durability.

Library of Congress Cataloging-in-Publication Data

Names: Neal, Bill, 1936- author. Title: Death on the lonely Llano Estacado : the assassination of J.W. Jarrott, a forgotten hero / by Bill Neal. Description: Denton, TX : University of North Texas Press, [2017] | Includes bibliographical references and index. Identifiers: LCCN 2017017335 | ISBN 9781574416954 (hardcover) Subjects: LCSH: Jarrott, J. W., 1861-1902--Assassination. | Lawyers--Texas--Biography. | Rural landowners--Texas--Biography. | Frontier and pioneer life--Llano Estacado. | Frontier and pioneer life--Texas--Lubbock County. | Texas--History--1846-1950.Classification: LCC F391.J37 N43 2017 | DDC 976.4/06092 [B] --dc23

LC record available at https://lccn.loc.gov/2017017335

Death on the Lonely Llano Estacado: The Assassination of J. W. Jarrott, a Forgotten Hero is Number 17 in the A.C. Greene Series

The electronic edition of this book was made possible by the support of the Vick Family Foundation.

Table of Contents

List of Figures

Acknowledgments

I had never heard of J. W. Jarrott. Never heard of the heroic role Jim Jarrott played in leading the first band of homesteaders to stake their claims on the vast lonesome South Plains frontier—a land previously deemed uninhabitable, and a land where hostility awaited them. That is, I had never heard of the Jarrott story until I read my friend Chuck Lanehart's article entitled "A History Mystery: Who Shot J. W.?" in the May 2011 edition of the Voice for the Defense magazine. Chuck is not only a premier criminal defense lawyer in Lubbock, Texas, he is also one of the best grassroots historians who focuses on frontier history of the South Plains of El Llano Estacado.

Intrigued by the story of J. W. Jarrott, I told Chuck that his story was more than a magazine article—it merited a well-researched book. Chuck agreed but said his busy law practice made it impossible for him to undertake that task. That's when I asked him if I could seize the mantle and begin the research. This retired criminal lawyer itched to dive into researching and writing the J. W. Jarrott story. Chuck agreed and turned over his Jarrott files to me, and has subsequently assisted by reading and correcting my drafts and suggesting areas for further research.

And so to Chuck Lanehart: "Thank you. Thank you very much."

Help also came from another noted South Plains historian: John Hope of Levelland. To say that John is a talented and meticulous historian is a gross understatement of his talents and expertise. He and his wife, Bette, are awesome musicians and artists, and John also teaches art at South Plains Junior College. Moreover, John has conducted narrated historical tours of the South Plains and furnished tour members a guidebook entitled *Texas' Last Frontier Ranch Heritage Tour*, and is made up of sixty-six pages chock full of historical research. John Hope has drawn two well-researched maps of the area, including locations of 1902 ranch headquarters, homesteader locations, and exactly where important incidents in the Jarrott story took place. To John and his wife, Bette Hope: "Mucho gracias."

Finally I must give credit for much invaluable research provided to me by the noted Wild West historian Ellis Lindsey of Waco, Texas, the fruits of which I have woven into the Jarrott story—especially in telling the background of Deacon Jim (also accurately called "Killin' Jim") Miller, whose career tragically intersected that of J. W. Jarrott. Thank you very much, Ellis.

Next I must extend a well-deserved "thank you" to my wife and companion, Gayla Neal, who is also my secretary, my research assistant, and the doer of all manner of other unglamorous tasks.

Valuable research resources also include Tai Kreidler, Monte Monroe, Lynn Whitfield, and other staff at the Southwest Special Collections Library at Texas Tech University; Warrren Stricker, research center director at the Panhandle-Plains Historical Museum; as well as Donaly E. Brice and John Anderson at the Texas State Library. Thanks also to H. Allen Anderson and the staff at The New Handbook of Texas of the Texas State Historical Association, and to the staff of the Haley Memorial Library and History Center at Midland, Texas. Much appreciation also to Ron Chrisman and his staff at the University of North Texas Press for their help and encouragement.

Foreword

The Lubbock bar has a quaint tradition, unique among bar associations in Texas. When a local lawyer dies the bar meets at the courthouse to remember, honor, and often roast the fallen warrior. I relish the chance to attend every such memorial. There is always a bit of wisdom, a nugget of humor, a hint of history, and always the chance a universal truth will be discovered here.

From as far back as I can remember, the local bar president stands and solemnly announces a tradition that dates back to 1902, "when the first of our memorial services was held to honor Lubbock lawyer J. W. Jarrott, the victim of a contract killing." A lawyer killed? Victim of a contract killing? In Lubbock County—when only 300 souls called it home? Must've been quite a scandalous story, I thought. Deserves some looking into.

So I poked around a bit, trying to shed some light on what turned out to be the oldest unsolved crime of the Texas South Plains. But I kept bumping into brick walls. Eventually, I presented my findings and many questions to fellow lawyer-historian Bill Neal. Intrigued, my friend Bill took the bull by the horns, and the result is this wonderful book.

In his many acclaimed works, Bill demonstrates a special talent for recounting small dramas of the Old West, retelling true tales that resonate with modern readers. His role is usually the colorful narrator of fascinating stories like those in *Getting Away with Murder on the Texas Frontier*, his classic from a few years back. Here, with the saga of James W. Jarrott, Bill undertakes a new role: detective/special prosecutor. Bill's distinguished background as a trial lawyer helps him unravel the many legal twists and turns involved in the Jarrott story.

The result is a delightful variation on the familiar dime novel theme of small farmers and settlers challenging entrenched large cattle ranchers for prime agricultural land, which forms the backdrop to the Jarrott true-life murder mystery. What emerges from these pages is the strength of intriguing characters as they come to life under Bill's careful analysis:

Jim Jarrott, the diminutive advocate who fearlessly champions the cause of the little guy; the Blankenship family, intrepid pioneers of the first order; the ruthless and slippery assassin, Deacon Jim Miller; the greedy and conniving Brownfield clan; and Jarrott's young widow, Mollie, who perseveres and prospers against great odds.

In our state, there is no statute of limitations for the offense of murder, but you can't indict someone who has been buried more than a century. Otherwise, with the findings illustrated here, Bill would have a few more convictions under his belt. He is to be commended for solid detective work coupled with brilliant writing that goes a long way in rectifying the Jarrott tragedy.

It becomes evident from Bill's chronicle that Jarrott's struggles and accomplishments rival those of his predecessor, Stephen F. Austin, the Father of Texas, whose name is reflected in our state capital and innumerable schools and public buildings. Just as Austin originally colonized the Mexican province of Texas, Jarrott colonized the South Plains of Texas, which now boasts cities and towns, major universities and colleges, a thriving oil industry, a huge medical center, and the largest contiguous cotton-producing region in the world. Many of Jarrott's descendants still call this place home, as do descendants of his clients, the original settlers of this region. Yet his name does not appear on a single place of honor anywhere on the South Plains.

If not for this important book, James W. Jarrott's legacy might have been lost forever.

Chuck Lanehart

Lawyer, Western Historian, Author

Lubbock, Texas, 2016

Prologue

August 1902. Jim Jarrott and wife, Mollie, walking down the main street of Lubbock, noticing a well-dressed gentleman staring at them from the opposite side of the road, Jim saying to Mollie: "There's a man I'd rather not see in this country."

The gentleman just stood there: motionless, expressionless, silent—studying Jim Jarrott, fixing him with cold, unblinking eyes, making no sign of recognition or greeting. After the Jarrotts passed, the handsome, well-groomed stranger turned and quietly disappeared.

Dedication

This book is dedicated to the memory of my grandfather, Will Neal (1874-1952), Oklahoma Territory cowboy and Texas pioneer rancher —another *"forgotten hero"* who deserved far more recognition than he ever received—or sought.

In 1897, on borrowed money, he burrowed a dugout into the banks of a creek along the western fringe of the expanding West Texas frontier and laid claim to the ranch where I grew up.

It took granddad almost half a century of daylight-to-dark hard work to support himself, his wife, and their four children, and to somehow come up with enough money to make those dreaded annual mortgage payments on the ranch—this was despite several crashes in the cattle market, droughts, tick-fever cattle quarantines, and especially the double-whammy of that God-awful decade of the 1930s with the national economic Depression and the terrible dust-bowl days on the Great Plains —the time it never rained.

Yet somehow, and without seeking or receiving aid from the government, granddad Will Neal rode through the thickets of life and left a ranch for his family, as well as a rich heritage for his family and his community.

Figure 1. Will Neal and author Bill Neal.

(Author's collection.)

Will Neal and his grandson, author Bill Neal, "ridin' the range" on the Neal Ranch, Hardeman County, Texas, circa 1938.

Preface

The passage of the Four-Sections Act "...set off an influx of settlers fanning out through the large ranches, in decrepit wagons, often containing their families, all their earthly goods, and pulled by tired plow teams. However objectionable it was to cattlemen [who were pasturing their herds on thousands of acres of unfenced range land] the Act, more than any other factor, brought about the settlement of West Texas."[1]

The Four-Sections Act provided that any adult Texan could purchase four sections of land (each section consisting of 640 acres and encompassing one square mile) from the state of Texas for one dollar an acre, and that was payable over forty years.

In the winter of 1901 and spring of 1902, J. W. Jarrott's band of twenty-five homesteader families, "nesters" as they were called, loaded their families and all their earthly possessions in a covered wagons, hitched up their teams and headed West for the promised land, the sprawling mostly uninhabited prairies on El Llano Estacado.[2]

Figure 2. Homesteader Wagon

(Sketch by Jimmy Clay. Author's collection.)

Death on the Lonely Llano Estacado

Chapter 1

The Precipice

> Inside the prairie schooner Mary Blankenship froze in terror and clasped her six-month-old baby to her breast as the wagon wheels inched ever closer to the edge of the precipice. She dared not look down at the yawning canyon floor; there, far below, it patiently awaited their arrival...their eternity. [1]

It had taken the homestead seekers—Andrew and Mary Blankenship and their baby, traveling in the lead wagon with Solon Cowan and Griff Hiser in the second—two weeks of hard, slow going, first near their tree-shaded home territory, fording flowing streams, and then into West Texas where the landscape changed. Drastically. Their wagons bumped over and around the rough, broken, and eroded red clay terrain of dry gullies, shallow canyons, and low cedar-splotched mesas to reach the precipitous Caprock escarpment, above which lay their destination: El Llano Estacado, the Staked Plains.

January 8, 1902. At the foot of the escarpment they had reined their mules to a halt and stared in awe and dismay at the almost vertical stone wall that in places soared to a height of 300 feet: layer upon layer of residue which, over eons of time and tides, had accumulated and fossilized. Winding up the escarpment was a steep, rocky, and narrow wagon trail that was hardly reassuring and seemed, in fact, to dare mere mortals to try it.

Then the weather turned against them.

A frigid, dust-laden, dry January norther swept down from the high plains and met them head-on, the cold blasts blowing into the open front of the covered wagons and swelling the canvas covers until the prairie schooners looked like giant balloons. [2] At that point the home-seekers wisely decided to join forces and attempt the ascent one wagon at a time —the Blankenship wagon going first.

Slowly they climbed higher. Halfway up, the trail narrowed, the wind got colder and more violent, and the mules got more stubborn, and when the winding trail turned once again, the winter blasts hit the wagon broadside and that's when it began its terrifying skid toward the brink of the canyon. Toward the brink of eternity. While inside the prairie schooner Mary froze in terror clutching her baby, outside Andy and the two fellow homesteaders fought desperately to avoid the yawning chasm of disaster. Andy lashed the stubborn mules, their heads lowered, both straining against gravity and the norther's frigid gale to pull the heavy load up the steep trail; the other two men struggled to pry the front wagon wheels inward and guide them away from the precipice.

Mary: "I tried not to see our predicament or hear the deafening shouts of the men as they maneuvered the team and wagon." [3]

Slowly. Very slowly the three struggling men and the two reluctant mules climbed...inch by inch... foot by foot... until at last they finally reached the top of that long and treacherous trail up the escarpment. Then they stopped. And, once again, they stared in awe at what they beheld. There, stretched before them—stretched to infinity it seemed—was a boundless, treeless, uninhabited ocean of grass that rolled on and on to the distant horizon where it melded into the western sky. A vast melancholy land where there was nothing to cast a shadow.

When the dry blizzard abated and the dust settled, they sensed another presence as real as it was invisible: silence. Silence—heavy, oppressive, and eternal—days on end of unbroken silence which, when coupled with the everlasting wind and the emptiness of the plains, evolved into a solitude tinged with sadness. Especially for the women. Years later, Mary Blankenship reflected: "We all had heard of the loneliness of the country in which we were to make our stand to live and die." But the stark reality of that lonely land they now beheld overwhelmed what mere words could never convey. "In just eight days, old things had passed away, and all things had become new...we had stepped over the threshold into a new world." [4]

Mary Blankenship was the first pioneer woman to make her home—a tent, as it were—on the South Plains of El Llano Estacado. [5] She, her husband, Andy, and their baby boy were among the first of twenty-four hardscrabble, rural settlers who had uprooted, loaded all their dreams and earthly possessions into a covered wagon, and headed west. These twenty-four "nester" families had trusted and relied upon the reassurance of their leader, James William Jarrott, the young lawyer who had surveyed and then staked out homestead tracts on those uninhabited plains southwest of the tiny village of Lubbock, Texas. Jim Jarrott was the only one of the pioneers who had actually seen the home sites—or the Llano Estacado itself, for that matter—before the settlers made that life-changing decision to stake their futures on the new frontier. Jim Jarrott and his wife, Mollie, also staked a homestead, thus bringing the total to twenty-five claims.

Loneliness was not the only problem the homesteaders faced. They had no preconceived illusions that their lives would be easy on this semiarid, windswept wilderness where there were no trees nor any flowing rivers or streams. Many of their neighbors who were back home in their safe, tree-shaded world predicted that they would return, tails tucked between their legs, within three months—a year tops.[6] The pioneers also realized that their very survival on this new frontier depended on daily, daylight-to-dark drudgery, or, as Mary Blankenship later put it in a colloquial expression of the time, it was "root-little-hog-or-die." [7]

Those nester settlers did not, however, anticipate another life-threatening danger that they all would soon face. One that no one had warned them about. One that was lurking just ahead. Out there on the lonely Llano Estacado.

Chapter 2

El Llano Estacado

> "I traveled...until I reached some plains, with no more landmarks than as if we had been swallowed by the sea."

So reported Francisco Vasquez De Coronado after crossing El Llano Estacado in 1541 in search of the fabled "Seven Cities of Cibola."[1] He found neither gold nor water on that featureless sea of grass.

In 1820, almost three centuries after Coronado, Major Stephen H. Long, a member of the US Corps of Topographical Engineers, was dispatched to make a scientific investigation. "The Great American Desert," was the way Maj. Long described what he found. It was an epithet that was accepted and perpetuated for years by civilized folks back East. During his trek across the plains Maj. Long also encountered a camp of Kiowa-Apache Indians who the major pronounced "the most degraded and miserable Indians" in the West—inhospitable savages living in an inhospitable land, Maj. Long concluded.[2]

A few years later, in 1849, US army captain Randolph B. Marcy led an expedition across what he called "the dreaded Llano Estacado...the great Zahara of North America." Marcy's report continued:

> It is a region almost as vast and trackless as the ocean—a land where no man, either savage or civilized, permanently abides; it spreads forth into a treeless, desolate waste of uninhabited solitude, which always has been, and must continue, uninhabited forever...[3]

Marcy's prediction was wrong. The "great Zahara" was to become Texas' last frontier.

El Llano Estacado, the Staked Plains—the southern extension of America's Great Plains—a vast windswept and semiarid mesa sprawling over more than 30,000 square miles. It straddles the Texas-New Mexico border, and its land mass exceeds the combined size of seven of the original thirteen states of the United States. The Canadian River at the top of the Texas Panhandle marks the northern boundary of El Llano Estacado, and then to the south it extends 250 miles into West Texas to the edge of the Edwards Plateau and the town of Odessa. The Mescalero Escarpment, just east of the Pecos River in New Mexico, is the western boundary, and the plains sweep eastward 150 miles to the steep canyon escarpment formed by the headwaters of the Red, Pease, Brazos, and Colorado Rivers in Texas. Llano Estacado is the tableland remnant from the apron of outwash that stretches eastward following the uplift of the Rocky Mountains some seventy million years ago.[4]

ANGLO SETTLEMENT

Until well after the Civil War there was no settlement on El Llano Estacado. It was the domain of the buffalo, the Apache (and later the Comanche), and the Kiowa. At the conclusion of the Red River War in 1874, the Indians were driven off the plains of Texas and onto Oklahoma reservations, and by the early 1880s hunters had slaughtered most of the buffalo herd. Thereafter, a few cattle ranchers began to stake out big spreads in the northern portion of El Llano Estacado. Charles Goodnight drove the first herd of cattle to the Palo Duro Canyon in the Panhandle of Texas in 1875.[5] Settlement didn't really boom, however, until the Fort

Worth & Denver City Railroad crossed the Texas Panhandle in 1888. Amarillo became the commercial hub on the North Plains area.

Figure 3. Map "El Llano Estacado"

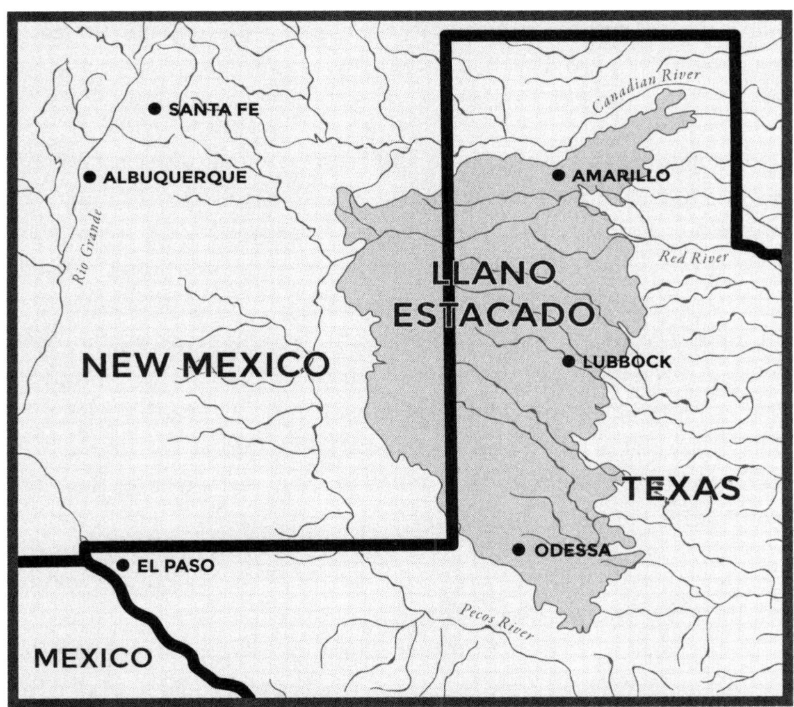

(Author's collection.)

It would be more than two decades before any railroad extended its line to the town of Lubbock, establishing it as the commercial hub of the South Plains. (The North Plains of Texas—the Panhandle—consists of twenty counties. The South Plains of Texas consists of the seventeen counties adjacent to, and south of, the North Plains.) The sparse population of the South Plains didn't justify the cost of building a railroad until 1909. The

1900 federal census revealed that the county of Lubbock was populated by only 293 hardy pioneers. Four counties, Hockley, Cochran, Terry, and Yoakum, all lying west of Lubbock County, were even more sparsely populated, each having less than 100 inhabitants. Moreover, none of those counties were "organized" counties, meaning that they had no county government, no county seat town, and no judicial system. All these counties were attached to nearby organized counties for local governmental and judicial services.

Settlement on the South Plains had been slow not only because there was no railroad lines connecting it to the rest of America, but also because out there on that flat sea of grass there was little wood or water. Although there were no flowing creeks or rivers providing a reliable source of water on the South Plains, it was discovered in the mid-1880s that there was an enormous sea of fresh water lying only about 120 feet or less below that sea of grass—the Ogallala Aquifer. The big ranchers solved their water problem by digging wells and erecting towering forty-foot Eclipse windmills about every four miles across the prairie. (The cattlemen knew that their cattle would graze up to two miles from their water source but no farther.)

With water available, those unfenced miles of protein-rich prairie, buffalo, and gramma grasses turned into a beef bonanza for large operators—free grass. At least, as it turned out, parts of those thousands of acres of that rangeland were free grass, and the rest could be leased from the State of Texas for a few cents per acre. Under those circumstances, there was really no incentive for any rancher to buy land from the state. Nevertheless, the owner of one ranch—and it was a very, very large ranch —did own the land. It was the three-million-acre XIT Ranch, granted to the owner by the Texas Legislature. Unlike any other state in the United States, Texas actually owned the land within its borders. The land ownership was reserved to the state by the 1845 annexation treaty between the United States and the independent Republic of Texas when

Texas joined the union. The State of Texas, therefore, enacted its own land development and homestead laws.

In 1879, the State of Texas was in dire need of a new state capitol building in Austin—the old capitol building having burned down. But there was a problem. Texas was broke. The state may not have had any spare money, but it did have an enormous amount of unsettled land available. In 1882, the Texas Legislature awarded a Chicago consortium, "the Capitol Syndicate," a 3,050,000-acre land grant in consideration for the construction of a red granite state capitol building—a frontier skyscraper 311 feet high, taller even than the US Capitol. The impressive edifice still, to this day, graces the capitol complex in Austin.[6]

Figure 4. State Capitol, Austin Texas – Front 1906

(Public Domain. Historic Texas Postcards, George Fuermann "Texas and Houston" Collection, Special Collections, University of Houston Libraries.)
When the Texas capitol in Austin was destroyed by fire in 1881, the state was cash poor but land rich. To finance the building of a new capitol the state granted a Chicago syndicate 3,050,000 acres of land along the western edge of the Texas Panhandle and South Plains in exchange for construction of a new capitol building.

And that was how the Capitol Syndicate earned ownership of the vast XIT Ranch, which extended some two hundred miles north-to-south along the western edge of the Texas-New Mexico border, all the way from the northwest corner of the Texas Panhandle down to its southern boundary near the present location of Levelland, Texas, and about thirty miles west of Lubbock. The XIT thus came to own a sizeable part of the north half of Hockley County, Texas—a fact that was to become important to this story when two decades later, J. W. Jarrott and his band of homesteaders began staking claims in the southern part of Hockley County.

THE FOUR-SECTIONS ACT

The passage of the Four-Sections Act in 1895, as amended in 1897, was a watershed event in Texas history.[7] Until 1891 executive and legislative sympathy in Austin had favored large ranching interests, railroads, and corporations. That changed with the election of Populist governor James S. Hogg, who took office in January 1891. He was succeeded by the election of another Populist governor: Charles A. Culberson, who held that office from 1895 until January 1899. By the passage of the Four-Sections Act, the Texas legislature signaled a reversal of sympathy in favor of the farmer-stockman and a growing number of rural pilgrims such as small town developers, merchants, schoolteachers, and religious leaders as well as homesteaders.

More than any other factor, the passage of the Four-Sections Act brought about the settlement of West Texas. Pursuant to that legislation a genuine Texas homesteader (not a land speculator) could purchase four sections of land under very favorable terms. As noted previously in the preface, Panhandle pioneer James D. Hamlin, "The Flamboyant Judge," commenting on the effect that the passage of this act had on the settlement of the Panhandle area in the North Plains, said that it "set off an influx of settlers fanning out through the large ranches." Settlement under the Four-Sections Act progressed at a faster pace on the North Plains than on the South Plains, and this was because by 1888 the North

Plains had a railroad, the Fort Worth and Denver City Railroad, that traversed it East to West. On the other hand the South Plains had no railroad until 1909. That retarded Four-Section Act settlers considerably. For instance, a Four-Sections Act settler who staked his claim west of Lubbock had to travel by horse and wagon 110 miles to the southeast to reach the Texas and Pacific Railroad station at the town of Big Spring for food, supplies, and markets. This round trip took up to fourteen days, or even longer if it snowed and obliterated the wagon trail. If that happened the homesteader had to hunker down and wait for a thawing to uncover the wagon trail across that sea of grass so he could continue his journey home.[8]

After the Civil War, the State of Texas still retained ownership of almost all of the unsettled lands in the western part of the state. In addition to the Four-Sections Act, the Texas legislature, in a further effort to encourage settlement and development of the state, had designated a large portion of these state lands as either "school lands" or "railroad lands." The object of a "railroad land" designation was to encourage settlement of West Texas by the construction of railroads. The state granted title to sixteen sections of land in favor of any railroad as a reward for constructing one mile of railroad track. On the other hand, the proceeds from the sale or lease of "school lands" went back into the Texas treasury and were designated for the support of education in the state. And, unlike "railroad" sections, "school" sections could be sold to individuals (provided they were Texans), and the four-section homesteaders eagerly seized upon the opportunity to finally realize their share of the American dream: own their own piece of land, start their own business, become their own boss, and, hopefully, become prosperous.

"THE STRIP"

In both the North Plains and the South Plains of El Llano Estacado, the cattle kings were reluctant to form a welcoming committee to greet these "nesters"—at least not a "friendly" welcoming committee. In the South

Plains there was another factor that sparked additional friction between the two groups. It was discovered in about 1900 that the state's original surveyors had made a serious error when they surveyed the South Plains, resulting in a large north-to-south unsurveyed gap between the official survey lines. That, in turn, resulted in a vacancy of land ownership or right of possession under a state lease—a no-man's slice of land that extended east to west from the west line of Lubbock County all the way, a distance of sixty miles in length, to the New Mexico border, and north to south a distance of two-and-a-half to five miles in width. "The Strip," as it became known, included the southern edges of Hockley and Cochran Counties and the northern edges of Terry and Yoakum Counties. (See Map: "The Setting," chapter four showing location of "The Strip.") All told, that unfenced vacancy covered several hundred thousand acres, all of which had been utilized by adjoining ranchers, albeit unwittingly, as free grasslands. The vacancy was discovered by J. W. Jarrott's friend and former Texas legislator, Charles Rogan, who was then serving as the commissioner of the Texas General Land Office in Austin. Commissioner Rogan tipped off friend Jarrott to his discovery.

Settlement of that unsurveyed strip would be facilitated by another factor: none of the tracts within the strip had been designated as "railroad land" and thus set aside for the construction of railroads. Therefore, Land Commissioner Rogan was free to classify all strip land as "school land" and then place it on the market to homesteaders pursuant to the Four-Sections Act. When J. W. Jarrott became aware of this unsurveyed vacancy soon to be designated as "school" land, he lost no time plucking that ripe, low-hanging fruit dangling right in front of him. J. W. Jarrott set about the task of enlisting twenty-five homesteaders to settle on 100 sections of land (64,000 acres) on the eastern end of the strip in southern Hockley and northern Terry Counties.

J. W. Jarrott's active role in seizing the opportunity to promote the settlement of this large slice of no-man's land (including a Four-Section claim for himself and his wife, Mollie) further aggravated South Plains cattle barons who already resented any intrusion on "their" turf by anyone—particularly "nesters."[9]

Chapter 3

Stepping Over the Threshold

> Nostalgia crept over us as we watched the cedar covered mounds of hills behind us give way to this level plain land that had lured us away from our beloved woods, our home folks, and our comfortable living. In just eight days, old things had passed away and all things had become new. We suddenly realized that we were a very young group of pioneers removing ourselves by slow transportation and communication from our native habitat. None had experienced this new life before us. We had stepped over the threshold into a new world.
>
> **Mary Blankenship reminisces in "The West Is for Us: The Reminiscences of Mary A. Blankenship."[1]**

None of the prospective homesteaders who Jim Jarrott recruited to settle on "The Strip" had ever seen that wild, windswept, and unpopulated tableland on the South Plains of El Llano Estacado. Nevertheless, Andrew and Mary Blankenship were captivated by Jarrott's presentation, especially when he informed them that poor folks such as themselves could—on account of the recently enacted Four-Section law—actually acquire title to 2,560 acres of rich farm land for a total purchase price of only $1.00 per acre and that amount to be paid out over forty years with lenient terms, including only three percent interest. However, the settler was required to established a home on the property and live on it for at least three months during each of the first three years and make some improvements. The only immediate cost was the $24 filing fee.[2] (Jim Jarrott didn't charge any fee for his services.)

Tenant farmers such as the Blankenships who had never owned one acre of land were enthralled with the prospect of actually owning their own land—and a whopping 2,560 acres at that! Where they lived in the Stephenville area in north central Texas, the fields that they farmed on a sharecropping basis, which meant dividing the proceeds from the sale of the crop with the landowner. The landowners usually owned no more than forty, or eighty, or, at most, 160 acres. To actually own their own land, to become independent, to become masters of their own destiny, and to look forward to becoming prosperous, maybe even wealthy some day... well, that was more than they had ever dreamed possible.

Andrew and Mary Blankenship became determined to better their lives and fortunes on that new frontier.

Both Andrew and Mary were the hardy stock of impoverished and hardworking rural families whose children had never known leisure or luxury. Andrew was born in a log cabin near Stephenville in 1872. His family was a large one: he had six brothers, one sister, three half-sisters, and three half-brothers, all brought up scrambling for a vacant bed and a plate of food.

Mary Alma "Allie" Perritt, born in 1878 in Meridian, Bosque County, Texas, had had an even worse and more deprived childhood. She became an orphan at age four. Her mother, Mary Ann Richards Perritt, died when Mary was only two years old, leaving two younger siblings: William Hamp and Ella Ann, who was only eight days old when her mother died. Two years later Mary's father, William Wallace Perritt, died, leaving her maternal grandparents, then in their sixties, to rear the three toddlers. The grandfather, Stratford Wade Hampton Richards, lost his Louisiana plantation, his cotton gin, and his slaves after the Civil War. Afterward he migrated to Texas and became a traveling Baptist evangelist. His wife, Elander Caroline, was a mid-wife and prescription druggist.

Years later, in her 1958 memoirs, Mary Perritt Blankenship recalled that her maternal grandparents, the Richards, who raised her and her younger siblings after their parent's death "...were old and moved many times, so [that they] the orphaned children, received only crumbs from the table of education, although [grandfather Richards] talked with pride of his father's graduation [prior to the Civil War] from Lexington Military College, his Louisiana family of school teachers, and his being a Mason."[3]

There was little time for carefree fun and frolic in Mary's childhood. The orphan took on the yoke of long hours of hard work to maintain herself and her two younger siblings, and to relieve their aging grandparents, thus developing a hardscrabble foundation that would serve her well during her adult years as a pioneer on the West Texas frontier.

One day when Mary was seventeen years old, Mary's maternal grandfather, Hampton Richards, the traveling evangelist, and Andy's father, Joseph Benson Blankenship, were sitting on the "whittler's bench" in Stephenville visiting. They were close friends and Confederate veterans who had soldiered together during the Civil War. Granddad Richards was preparing to leave town the next day for a three-week revival, and told Mr. Blankenship that if he would allow Mary to stay at the Blankenship's home while he was away, Mary would serve as Mrs. Blankenship's maid. Mr. Blankenship agreed, and the next day he came after Mary in his buggy. He soon became much impressed with this attractive and intelligent young lady, and on the way to the Blankenship home he confidentially told Mary that she could "have her pick" to marry any one of his seven sons.

After Granddad Richards' three-week revival was over, Mary remained at the Blankenship home and helped the family pick cotton. That's where —in the cotton patch—she fell in love with Andy Blankenship. He was, as she later noted, "the pick of the litter." And so, one day, while she picked cotton, she also picked Andy.

Andy was twenty-three and Mary was seventeen when they got married on December 5, 1895. With fifteen borrowed dollars Andy and Mary bought a bedstead, a stove, two chairs, and a table. The bride had a few linens in her hope chest, and Andy owned one horse, fifty bushels of wheat, and fifty bushels of corn. Someone loaned the young couple a wooden bucket and a dipper.

They began their married life together in fields owned by others—sharecropping for a share of the profits, if any, or picking cotton for other farmers (they could each pick 300 pounds per day at 30 cents per hundredweight, thus netting them $1.80 per day), plus Andy chopped wood at 50 cents per cord, and they also did other field work. After three years of living with others (the homes of the farmers they worked for), they finally got to live in a house by themselves. It was an old and decrepit log cabin. Mary papered the walls with newspapers. Andy built a log rail fence around it. They planted a garden, bought a milk cow and several hens from which they hatched a flock. Soon they were able to trade butter, eggs, and vegetables in Stephenville for groceries. During their third year together Andy and Mary spent only $25 for living expenses.

On July 30, 1901, their first baby was born: Wallace Benson Blankenship.

A LIFE-ALTERING ADVENTURE BEGINS

The fall of 1901 was a busy one for the Blankenships. They devoted most of their time to preparing for their life-altering adventure. Realizing that once settled on their claim on those vast plains, they would be on their own and alone—miles from their nearest neighbor, a days horseback ride from the frontier village of Lubbock—and no means of communication, and no doctor available in event of a serious illness or an accidental injury. They attempted to anticipate and address whatever fate might have in store. Mary consulted a local doctor. Dr. Naylor coached her in home nursing: lancing sores, delivering and caring for babies, setting broken bones, and treating usual ailments. The doctor also recommended she take along basic home remedies such as calomel, paregoric, kerosene, Watkins liniment, and a quart of whiskey in case of a snakebite. Andy took lessons on animal care from the local veterinarian.

Then came the task of selecting which items to take and which to leave behind, choosing between the unnecessary and the indispensable. Whatever they selected to take had to fit within their fourteen-foot covered wagon. In addition to a few pieces of disassembled household furniture, they took bedding, clothing, a coffee grinder, a carpet beater, an iron wash pot, a coal oil lantern and lamp, two flat irons, quilting frames, a bachelor stove with a drum oven, crockery milk vessels, a butter churn, a forge for shaping tools, an ax, a grubbing hoe, a gun, and their new home—a tent. Other basic implements including a turning plow and a saddle were tied to the side of the wagon. Sufficient seeds for a garden and crops had to be included as well as canned foods containing enough sugar, flour, meal, coffee beans, and home-cured meat to last them for at least four months—even a couple of years, if necessary. Needless to add, the family Bible and a national Bellas Hess catalog were essential and were their only reading material. Hours of entertainment in their new prairie home would be spent thumbing through the catalog until some years later when they received a new Sears Roebuck catalog, whereupon the old catalog was assigned to outhouse duties.

The last task before packing to leave was to muster whatever money they could scrape together. That didn't take too long. When, at last, they counted all their cash it amounted to $300, $100 of which was credit extended by their friendly local grocer for egg money. Then they turned all their cash into $20 gold pieces, which Mary sewed into a money belt that she fastened around her waist under "many petticoats and a full skirt."

By Christmas day 1901, they finally had completed all their departure tasks, had their covered wagon packed, and were ready to go. They spent their final day celebrating the holiday with their families and had their pictures made..."just in case." Andrew was twenty-nine, Mary was twenty-three, and their baby son, Wallace Benson Blankenship, was six months old.

Before leaving they also bid adieu to close friends, most of whom had been their neighbors for years. Between themselves, their friends and neighbors whispered a prediction that when the harsh reality of their new home on that windswept, featureless, lonely prairie set in, their dream bubble would burst and the Blankenships would "throw in the towel" and be back home within a few months, tail tucked between their legs—back home to those comfortable tree-shaded hills and valleys, where green meadows nestled against the banks of flowing streams and rivers. Perhaps those neighbors harbored a streak of envy at the boldness and courage exhibited by Andy and Mary. Perhaps, secretly, they hoped their own reluctance to make such a bold move would ultimately be vindicated—chalked up to wise caution rather than a lack of courage and determination.

The next morning the little family climbed into their prairie schooner, slapped the reins on the backs of their two mules, Jude and Kate, and they were off. The Blankenship's mare, Old Snide, trailed behind. Old Snide would serve as their spare mule just in case they lost one of the two mules en route. Beside the wagon, Old Dan, their faithful bird dog, trotted along. Another wagon followed them. Aboard were two other hopeful "Strip" settlers: Solon Cowan and Griff Hiser. The two-wagon caravan then turned their mules to the west. And the adventure began.[4]

If their stay-at-home neighbors dismissed Andy and Mary Blankenship as simply a starry-eyed young couple with fairy-tale dreams, who were beguiled and bedazzled by Jim Jarrott's rose-colored portrayal of the promised land awaiting them on the new frontier, they were wrong. If the neighbors believed that the harsh, unforgiving, and lonely life on the Llano Estacado would soon jar the young couple back to reality—and surrender—they were wrong.

Figure 5. Andrew "Andy" Blankenship and wife Mary and baby Wallace in 1901

(Public Domain. Courtesy of Southwest Collection/Special Collections Library, Texas Tech University, Lubbock, Texas. SWCPC Andrew, Mary, and Son Blankenship Papers.)

They traveled in a covered wagon to their new home on the Llano Estacado west of Lubbock in December 1901.

Seven years after their marriage, Andy and Mary Blankenship took Jim Jarrott up on his offer to help them stake a homestead claim on "The Strip." By then they had acquired at least a few more worldly goods and one baby—plus an abundant supply of grit, courage, and determination. Mary later wrote in her memoirs:

> My determination to rise above my childhood portion as an orphan since four years old was teamed with Andrew's frugality and inherent love of the land...we knew that with the earth bringing forth such increase, the Lord willing, we would someday be big farmers.[5]

Their determination would soon be severely tested, but as Mary later recalled: "If we had made our bed hard, we intended to lay on it."[6]

CHAPTER 4

J. W. AND MOLLIE JARROTT

> J. W. Jarrott was a trail-blazing lawyer and a courageous advocate...in the tradition of Stephen F. Austin, Jarrott brought some of the first waves of settlers to a vast wasteland once known as the Great American Desert, becoming a hero to his friends and clients, and then a martyr.

That was premier Lubbock criminal defense lawyer and author Chuck Lanehart's take on the brief, triumphant, yet tragic life of J. W. Jarrott.[1]

The backgrounds and personalities of the two young pioneer couples could hardly have been more diverse: Andy and Mary Perritt Blankenship, on the one hand, grim, serious-minded, and under-privileged children of large impoverished farm families, and on the other hand, James William Jarrott and Mollie Wylie Jarrott, the privileged, well-educated, articulate, and personable children of prominent families. Yet all four of these pilgrims shared some of the same qualities: they were all intelligent, adventurous, ambitious, hard-working, and bold risk-takers. Their lives and destinies would become intertwined on "the Strip." Out there on the lonely Llano Estacado.

Mollie D. Wylie was born April 27, 1866, in Hood County, Texas, just west of Fort Worth, and grew up in the family home at a tiny village named Thorp Spring. Her father, John N. M. Wylie, and maternal grandfather, Dr. Andrew Briggs, were prominent pioneer ranchers.[2] Every summer after Mollie became old enough to ride a horse, she mounted up, left the family home, and spent the entire summer on one of her father's ranches. He owned one ranch in Erath County near Stephenville and another in Runnels County on the Colorado River about fifty miles south of Abilene, Texas. Mollie's summer vacations were not devoted to fun and amusement—they were working vacations spent learning the ranching business, until, as her father phrased it, she was capable of "doing anything a rancher can do," which included shooting a rifle, branding cattle, and riding a horse "a-straddle," practices considered to be very unladylike in those times. (Ladies, in those Victorian tilted times, rode horses on sidesaddles.)[3] Life on the Texas frontier during those Reconstruction years after the Civil War was hard—difficult at best, even for adults. Mollie's youthful days were additionally burdened by the fact that she had to assume adult responsibility in helping care for her four younger siblings upon the premature death of their mother.[4] Nevertheless, it was a background that would later help sustain her through a very trying period of her life.

Mollie blossomed into a beautiful young lady with high cheekbones and black hair. She and her two brothers and two sisters all attended and graduated from Add-Ran College in Thorp Spring. (Add-Ran College was the forerunner of Texas Christian University and was relocated to Fort Worth.) While attending Add-Ran College, Mollie met a bright, ambitious, and charismatic young scholar named James William Jarrott, the son of Dr. Gardner Jarrott, a medical doctor. Abraham Lincoln was president of the United States when Jarrott, known as "J. W." or "Jim" by his close friends, was born on February 7, 1862, in Marion County, Alabama. The family escaped the ravages of the Civil War by moving to the frontier community of Millsap west of Fort Worth in Parker County, Texas.[5] Mollie Wylie and Jim Jarrott fell in love and were married on September

26, 1886. There exists only one known photograph of Jim Jarrott, a picture of him standing beside his beautiful young bride. The photograph depicts Jim Jarrott as somewhere between "plain" and "handsome."

J. W. JARROTT'S POLITICAL CAREER

In 1886, after graduating from college, J. W. and Mollie moved to Weatherford in Parker County, Texas, a few miles west of Fort Worth. There he met and was befriended by a local attorney, S. W. T. Lanham, who was then the US Congressman for the "Jumbo" 11th Congressional District consisting of ninety-eight sparsely populated Texas counties, and who later served as governor of Texas from 1903 until 1907.[6] Congressman Lanham offered Jarrott a position on his staff in Washington, but Jarrott, then only twenty-four years old, declined the offer, and instead decided to throw his own hat into the ring for a seat in the Texas Legislature representing Parker County. He won the race, and on January 11, 1887, Jim Jarrott took his seat in the Texas House of Representatives during its twentieth session. A sketch found in the personnel file of the Texas state government for that legislative session had this to say about J. W. Jarrott:

> The Honorable J. W. Jarrott is the most youthful looking member of the body... and is quite active and successful in his line of life... He has been prompt in his work of the Legislature and is fearless in speech. In the purposes he undertakes to carry out, he is persistent to the last. He shows quickness of discernment and a readiness to take hold of the best interests of the people whom he serves and represents. His labors in the committee room and in the hall, have been respected and given due consideration.
>
> J. W. Jarrott was married to Miss Mollie D. Wylie, of Parker County. He is a member of the Christian Church. He shows a commendable degree of cultivation, and is refined in his manners, small in stature, and of light figure; his action is quick, and his speech rather rapid.[7]

Figure 6. James "J. W." and Mollie Jarrott

(Public Domain. Courtesy of Southwest Collection/Special Collections Library, Texas Tech University, Lubbock, Texas. SWCPC 326-E 34)

J. W. Jarrott, a former Texas legislator, was the leader of the "nesters" who filed homestead claims on the South Plains at the turn of the twentieth century. After his assassination his wife Mollie seized the reins and encouraged the other nesters to "stay put."

The first session of the twentieth legislature lasted only three months—January 11, 1887-April 4, 1887. For reasons never revealed, when the first session ended Jarrott resigned. That Jarrott was restless, ambitious, and adventuresome is beyond dispute. Perhaps he succumbed to the siren call of a new adventure. Whatever the reason, in the fall of 1887, he and his father filed on a tract of land near Phoenix, Arizona. Mollie packed up and followed, and it was there that their first child, Elizabeth, was born.

The allure that had attracted him to the Arizona adventure soon faded, and the Jarrotts returned home to Texas in 1889, and settled in Stephenville, the county seat of Erath County. J. W. studied law in the office of an esteemed state district judge, Thomas Lewis Nugent, a vocal populist advocate.[8] Although Jarrott had never darkened the door of a law school, Judge Nugent, in 1894, swore him in as a member of the Texas Bar. His interest in politics was rekindled, and he quickly put his new law license to good use. He was named city attorney of Stephenville. The following year he ran for the office of county attorney of Erath County as a populist on the People's Party ticket and was elected. Jarrott, always a champion of the "little" people, caught the rising tide of populist sentiment in the 1895 race. He was reelected two years later. However, the populist tide had begun to ebb the next time he ran for reelection, and he was defeated.[9] As noted earlier, the Populist-era in Texas politics peaked during the four-year terms of Texas governors James S. Hogg and Charles A. Culberson, extending from 1891 through 1899.

During those years at Stephenville, three more children were born to Jim and Mollie: Mary, who died at age four as a result of an accidental fall in the family home, Richard, and John. After his defeat for reelection as county attorney, the Jarrott family was in dire financial straits. Years later, Mollie recalled that she encouraged her husband to run for another political office, but he refused, grumbling that all politics were corrupt.[10] Once again, the restless J. W. began looking beyond distant horizons for new opportunities.

In early 1900, he made his first excursion to the South Plains. He visited family friends, Lewis and Blanche Faulkner, who had relocated to Plainview, Texas. There he first became intrigued by stories of that vast unfenced and unpopulated Llano Estacado frontier. Fifty miles south of Plainview was located the tiny village of Lubbock, the county seat of Lubbock County.

The year 1900 would be pivotal in the lives and careers of J. W. and Mollie Jarrott. It was during that year that J. W. heard from an old friend and a former fellow Texas legislator named Charles Rogan who had recently been appointed by Texas governor Joseph Sayers to fill a vacancy as head of the state's General Land Office (GLO). Rogan, who was one of the first six graduates of Texas A&M University, later graduated from Harvard Law School. Afterward he returned to Texas and opened his own law office sixty miles southwest of Weatherford in the town of Brownwood where he was subsequently elected to the Texas House of Representatives.[11]

Jarrott's interest in the opportunities on the Texas South Plains had been sparked initially during his visit with the Faulkner family. But now, later that same year, the message he received from his friend, Texas land commissioner Charles Rogan, turned that spark into a flame. It was that message from Rogan that would prove to have a life and career altering impact on the future of J. W and Mollie Jarrott...and on the history of the South Plains of Texas.

Land Commissioner Rogan disclosed that in examining the Texas land records, he had discovered a strip of state-owned land that had never been surveyed—a sixty-mile long slice of land on the South Plains west of Lubbock County. He also disclosed that as land commissioner he intended to place it on the market for sale to settlers under the lenient terms of the state's Four-Sections Act. J. W. Jarrott wasted no time in devising a settlement plan that would take advantage of Commissioner Rogan's program. Jarrott reckoned that he knew just the place where he could find plenty of "nester" candidates among his populist sharecropper friends who would be eager to fill that vacuum.

SETTLEMENT OF "THE STRIP" BEGINS

However, before Rogan could place the land within "the Strip" on the market, it had to be surveyed. Apparently J. W. Jarrott was the first person—and the only person—who Rogan notified at that time about his discovery of this unsurveyed acreage, and that he intended to place it on the market when the survey was completed. It was necessary not only that the survey define the outer boundaries of the Strip, but that it also define the internal boundaries of each individual section within the Strip. To accomplish this, Rogan appointed an official surveyor named Mark Ragsdale, who hailed from Rogan's hometown of Brownwood. Ragsdale's total fee for the survey amounted to $3,000. While Rogan was waiting for the Texas legislature to appropriate Ragsdale's fee, J. W. Jarrott put up a "good faith" deposit of $500 to kick-start the survey. The survey was completed in the spring of 1902. The legislature appropriated funds for Ragsdale's $3,000 fee, and Commissioner Rogan refunded Jarrott's $500 deposit, and gave him a copy of the survey, which described not only the Strip's external boundaries but also each individual tract within. Ragsdale's survey verified that the vacancy did, in fact, exist and that it extended sixty miles, east to west, from the western boundary line of Lubbock County all the way to the New Mexico border, and it varied in width at different points along the way from two and one-half miles to five miles.[12]

Figure 7. "The Setting" for this story's location on the South Plains of Texas, circa 1902.

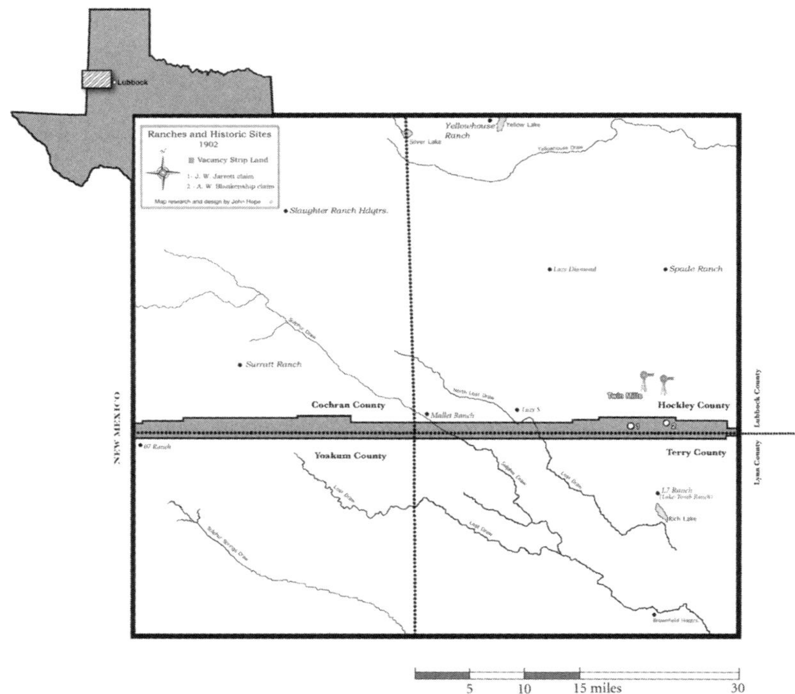

(Map drawn by John Hope. Author's collection.)

South Plains historian and artist John Hope has researched and captured on the above map when and where the key events described in this book occurred, including the location of the headquarters of the large ranchesand the location of the unsurveyed strip of land where J. W. Jarrott and his settlers began staking their Four-Section claims. Jarrott claim location noted #1 and Blankenship claim #2.

In the meantime, while Ragsdale was completing the survey, Jarrott returned to the Stephenville area where he and Mollie found a receptive audience, including Andrew and Mary Blankenship. Also expressing a keen interest were two young, unmarried, schoolteacher sisters, Florence and Louise Watkins, both of whom taught classes at John Tarleton College in Stephenville. They asked, "Are we really eligible to file claims out there?" Without hesitation, J. W. replied, "Of course! Both of you are over twenty-one, aren't you? But there are a lot of snakes out there!" Mollie chimed in, "If you girls are brave enough to go, then so am I."[13] Both women signed on. They, together with the Blankenships, would join the first wave of Strip claimants.

Each section contained 640 acres, and each claimant looked forward to owning four sections totaling 2,560 acres—an enormous plantation-sized plot of land in the minds of Erath County inhabitants accustomed to farms of 160 acres or less. All twenty-five of the first wave of Jarrott's homesteaders designated J. W. as their attorney (no attorney's fee charged), thus enabling Jarrott to enter bids not only for himself and Mollie, but also for all of his settler clients.

Land Commissioner Charles Rogan set April 24, 1902, as the date when the first nine settler applications would be accepted. Applications for purchase were to be taken on a "first-come-first-serve" basis at the county clerk's office in Lubbock and accepted at 8:00 a.m. on that date, and then forwarded to the General Land Office in Austin for approval. Rogan officially designated all land within the Strip as "school lands," meaning that all the proceeds from the sale of these tracts would be placed in the state's school fund. None of the Strip tracts were designated as "railroad lands," a fact that allowed Rogan to put all Strip acreage on the market for direct sale to individuals.

Although Rogan placed a notice of the intended land sale in the state's large daily newspapers some two weeks before April 24, 1902, and a copy of Ragsdale's survey was available to all interested parties at the General Land Office in Austin, still Jarrott had a distinct advantage when that date arrived. There were no daily newspapers published at that time on the South Plains, and apparently the big ranchers were caught napping. None of them requested a copy of Ragsdale's survey from the General Land Office. Consequently, only Jarrott had a copy of the survey giving a detailed description of the outer and inner boundary lines, including an identification of each of the individual sections up for grabs.[14]

Meanwhile, Jarrott had also set in motion an auxiliary plan to facilitate his main plan of settlement. About a year prior to the filing of his clients' claims on the Strip, he had located four sections of available land in Terry County several miles southeast of the Strip. Since these four sections were not located in the Strip and had already been surveyed, they were available for purchase prior to the sale of the Strip lands. J. W. managed to secure title for his brother, Ward Jarrott, and Ward followed through with the plan by digging a dugout there and establishing his residence. Consequently, when J. W.'s colony of nesters began moving their prairie schooners onto El Llano Estacado, Ward Jarrott's tract served as a gateway for J. W.'s Strip claimants. The settlers promptly christened Ward's dugout as their "community house." It was there that the first nine settlers waited while Jarrott set about physically staking out each of their individual homestead boundaries on the prairie, and then preparing the paperwork to file on each claim so that in April he would be ready to file and process their claims and win approval from the General Land Office in Austin.[15] The Blankenships, for example, arrived at Ward Jarrott's dugout on January 2, 1902, but were obliged to wait there for more than three months while J. W. was staking out individual claim boundaries prior to the April 24 filing date. It was that spring at Ward Jarrott's "community house" where the little band of settlers bonded together in anticipation, excitement, and friendship.

Back in Stephenville, when the spring school term ended in May 1902, Mollie and their three children, Elizabeth, John, and Richard, packed up all the family belongings and joined J. W. on the South Plains of Texas.

Chapter 5

Isolation, Loneliness... and Danger

> There were no bounds to the expanse before me. The land seemed to roll forever in swells of brown and gray. Never before had I felt so isolated and alone as I stood surrounded by miles upon miles of unbroken, barren plains.
>
> **Louis Fairchild, The Lonesome Plains: Death and Revival on an American Frontier.**[1]

Isolation, loneliness, and the fearful solitude of the vast plains tested the mettle of even the hardiest of J. W. Jarrott's band of settlers. But there were other daunting challenges just ahead.

Merely surviving with the limited resources and primitive tools available to them was a never-ending, daylight-to-dusk—"from-can-to-can't"—task for the homesteaders, or as Mary had so aptly summed it all up: it was a "root-litter-hog-or-die" existence,[2] complicated at times by nature in the form of droughts, blizzards, and the ever present dread of a wildfire raging unchecked across miles of tall prairie grass. Raging wildfires were feared by both ranchers and settlers, and they were common occurrences.

Jarrott's settlers along the Hockley County strip vividly recalled a huge blaze that started more than a hundred miles to the north and west and came roaring toward their homes. Smoke could be seen across the prairie for three days before it got to them. The settlers backfired a strip of grassland and saved their properties.[3] At least the daily struggle to survive occupied most of their time and served to alleviate the sieges of loneliness, solitude, and a sense of isolation—that plus the settlers' determination never to retreat, "to take our stand to live and die" on this frontier.[4]

In addition to the physical and emotional battles to survive in this new environment, the settlers soon became aware of another very formidable foe: the cattle barons. This became clear while the Blankenships and others in the first wave were marking time at Ward Jarrott's dugout waiting for J. W. Jarrott to file their homestead applications. In her memoirs Mary Blankenship recalled that J. W. frequently stopped to visit en route to the surveying missions required to stake their individual homestead boundaries on the Strip. After each visit he rode away, always astride Old Dick, his high-spirited black horse, and each time Mary recalled, "...we all breathed a prayer for his safe return. We sensed the opposition that existed because of his bringing us 'squatters' to intrude on 'their' turf."[5]

Finally Jarrott received official notice from the General Land Office (GLO) in Austin that application forms were being forwarded to the county clerk in Lubbock, and that April 24, 1902, had been designated as the date that four-section settlers on the Hockley County part of the Strip could file their claims. These completed applications would then be returned to Austin for final approval. Jarrott told these claimants that on the day before filing their applications it would be necessary for each of them to move some of their possessions onto their four-section tract and set up a tent. Accordingly, early on the morning of April 23, 1902, the first wave of claimants, J. W. Jarrott, Andrew Blankenship, Lee Cowan, Solon Cowan, Walter Frazier, G. M. Royalty, and John Doyle (who was to file his own claim plus claims for Louise and Florence Watkins), loaded their wagons and eagerly waited for Jarrott. It was overcast and cold when Jarrott arrived at their community camp. The parade of "squatters" then fell in line and followed. Only Jarrott knew where each claim was located on that vast sea of grass, and he led them to the far west end of their claims and then turned and came back east pausing briefly at each while the claimant pitched his tent. Then they proceeded on to the next homestead. It was dark when the last settler had pitched his tent. All the men, including Andy Blankenship, then mounted their horses and followed J. W. to Lubbock.

Mary and the baby together with an eight-year-old boy named Brock Gist were left alone to await the riders return after the applications had been completed and filed. (Gist was the son of one of Jarrott's other recruits who were scheduled to file their claims on the Terry County portion of the Strip.) Andy departed with the others riding Old Snide, leaving another horse, Old Duggan, tied to the wagon wheel. He also left the family shotgun and a five-gallon keg of water with Mary.

The next morning Mary cleared off a spot of grass and built a fire with the dried limbs of a mesquite scrub and cooked breakfast. By that afternoon they were out of water. She, the Gist boy, and Old Duggan were thirsty. The only sign of human habitation on the prairie was a windmill about one-and-a-half miles to the north located on the Lake Tomb (L7) ranch. Mary saddled Old Duggan, boosted Brock Gist aboard, and sent him off with the water keg. With the baby in her arms and the shotgun by her side, she leaned back against the wagon and anxiously watched as Brock and Old Duggan headed toward the distant windmill. She watched them all the way to the mill and back. It seemed like an eternity although it only took about two hours.

The settlers were aware that the ranchers had forbidden them access to their windmill water, but in those first few years the homesteaders had no other source. Mary later wrote:

> We realized that our settling meant an intrusion upon the cowmen's grazing range, but we had staked our lives here in the midst of their domain without even a fence to mark our own

> ground, and had no choice but to trespass as we gathered dry cow chips for wood and watered the horses and carried our water from their wells.[6]

Soon after Brock Gist returned with the water, Mary spied four horsemen approaching. She expected that they would come to the camp and exchange greetings. Instead, however, they circled around the camp several times at a distance glaring at them. It was obvious they had no intention of being neighborly. Shotgun in hand, Mary and the Gist boy stood by the wagon and watched.

The sun finally set. Darkness began to descend on the empty land. Loneliness tinged with fear set in. Then, at dusk, it got even worse. A lone coyote began to howl and soon was joined by others in a chorus of eerie wails. Mary fired the shotgun, but that only caused a temporary break. Then the cacophony resumed. Later that night the coyotes crept up to the campsite and managed to dig under an enclosure where Mary kept five hens. The critters ate two of them.

She got no rest that long sleepless night. Too scared to sleep in the tent, Mary, her baby, the Gist boy and the shotgun all huddled together inside the wagon. Would those cowboys attempt a night massacre?

The cowboys did not attempt a night raid, but the next afternoon the same four cowboys again appeared in the distance and again made that ominous ride around the camp. When Jarrott, Andy, and the other men had not arrived by dark that evening, Mary suspected that something had gone terribly wrong. Had the hostile cowboys ambushed the Jarrott homesteaders? But the cause of the delay was not nearly as serious as Mary had feared. The men's failure to return on schedule had been caused by a delay in mail service from Austin. The blank GLO application forms had been received in Lubbock a day later than expected. When the forms finally arrived in Lubbock, Jarrott and the homesteaders duly completed and signed the individual applications and posted them in the mail for approval by the GLO. Then they mounted and started for home.

Figure 8. Lubbock County Clerk's Office

(Public domain, Courtesy of Southwest Collection/Special Collections Library, Texas Tech University, Lubbock, Texas. SWCPC 57 – (U) E2.9)
In the town of Lubbock where J. W. Jarrott and his first group of settlers filed their homestead claims in April 1902.

Figure 9. Texas Land Grant Certificate

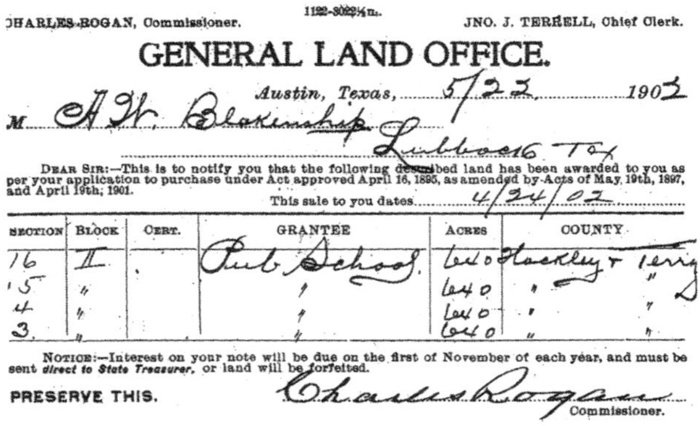

1122-3022½m.

CHARLES ROGAN, Commissioner. JNO. J. TERRELL, Chief Clerk.

GENERAL LAND OFFICE.

Austin, Texas, 5/22 1902

M A. W. Blankenship

Lubbock Tex

DEAR SIR:—This is to notify you that the following described land has been awarded to you as per your application to purchase under Act approved April 16, 1895, as amended by Acts of May 19th, 1897, and April 19th, 1901.

This sale to you dates 4/24/02

SECTION	BLOCK	CERT.	GRANTEE	ACRES	COUNTY
16	II		Pub School	640	Hockley & Terry
15	"		"	640	" "
4	"		"	640	" "
3	"		"	640	" "

NOTICE:—Interest on your note will be due on the first of November of each year, and must be sent *direct to State Treasurer*, or land will be forfeited.

PRESERVE THIS.

Charles Rogan
Commissioner.

(Public record.)
State of Texas Land Grant Certificate to A. W. Blankenship dated May 22, 1902, certifying his homestead claim to four sections (2,560 acres) of land on "The Strip" west of Lubbock.

Figure 10. Charles Rogan

(Public domain. "Cushing Memorial Library and Archives, Texas A&M University.")

Commissioner of the Texas General Land Office and a friend of J. W. Jarrott and his homesteaders. Rogan executed their "Four-Section" homestead certificates.

Meanwhile, Mary and Brock Gist spent another miserable night in camp alone...wondering, fearing. That night was even worse than the preceding night. A cold gale swept across the prairie, whipping their tent off its poles and leaving it in a tangled mess.

Late the next afternoon Jarrott, Andy, and their companions appeared on the horizon. Forgetting all about those freezing north winds, forgetting all about their tent lying in a frazzled heap, and forgetting all about the ominous tactics of the ranch cowboys, Mary and Brock Gist jumped up and down and whooped with joy at the welcome sight!

Then she laid the shotgun down.

Jim Jarrott and his merry band of homesteaders paused to celebrate with the Blankenships and to discuss plans for their future. Then they left. Mary and Andy sadly watched their dear friends and fellow homesteaders depart, leaving them all alone on the prairie. Mary also grieved as she watched Jim Jarrott take the Gist boy with him to be returned to his parents, reflecting that the "...brave little boy had become a man in the three days he had stayed with Wallace and me." In her memoirs, Mary added this observation: "Boys became men at an early age in this frontier."[7]

Still, Andy and Mary clasped each other and rejoiced. They were standing on their very own land—all 2,560 acres of it. What a long way they had come in such a short time!

But their struggles to survive and thrive on the lonely Llano Estacado were far from over.

SILENCE, ISOLATION, AND SOLITUDE

Solitude—anxious, fearful solitude!

Endless hours...days...weeks...ticked slowly by. Sometimes Mary Blankenship gazed across the boundless sprawl of prairie "swimming in a distant mirage that threatened to engulf us." And she wondered: are Andy and I the only people left inhabiting this earth?[8]

Their neighbors back home had forewarned Andy and Mary Blankenship that overwhelming isolation and loneliness lay in store for them at the end of the trail, and predicted that it would finally become unbearable and defeat them. And that prediction very nearly came true. Sometimes they almost panicked and gave up, almost tilted into packing up and retreating to those pleasant tree-shaded hills and flowing streams of home, and returning to neighbors to talk to.

Mary Blankenship: "We felt the absence of life on the Great Plains and were always starved for company and thirsty for conversation."[9] Sometimes Mary felt so lonely she found herself seeking the company of their cows. "I would go out to a watering hole and stroll among them, rubbing their hips, talking to them about their calves, asking questions which I knew they couldn't answer. Their contentment served as balm to my tense nerves."[10]

There was not one neighbor in sight of the Blankenship's crude half-dugout hut with its dirt floor. Lubbock, the nearest dot of habitation on the map was, in 1900, a tiny village with a population of only 117 inhabitants,[11] and that was a distance of a day's horseback ride away. (Distances in those times were not measured in miles, but in the length of time it took to ride a horse to the destination.)

Andy and Mary had no telephone, no newspaper, no radio, no television, no books (except the Bible and that National Bellas Hess catalogue), and no nearby school, church, or doctor to summon in case of an emergency. "No nothing," as one fellow pioneer summed it up, adding, "Women had terrible times in those days."[12]

Andy and Mary didn't even have a clock, a calendar, or a thermometer. She recalled:

> We studied the sky for weather signs, planted [our crops] and cut [castrated] our cattle by the moon signs, predicted the change of

> seasons by the flight of wild geese, told time of night by the cock's crow, told time of day by the sun, and [an approaching] wet spell by the falling of the smoke. We had no thermometer, but knew it was zero when we had to break a hole in the ice two or three times a day for the cattle to drink.[13]

Their "no nothing" list also included two other basic, essential and pressing needs: wood and water. There were no trees or sources of lumber with which to construct homes, barns or even fence posts; no wood or coal available for cooking or heating. Their only fuel was dried cow chips (manure) and the roots of spindly mesquite bushes. Their only source of water in the beginning was the "forbidden" water pumped by the Lake Tomb ranch windmill a mile and a half from their dugout. Mary quipped: "The wind draws our water, and the cows cut our wood."[14]

Figure 11. Dugout with dog

(Public Domain. Courtesy of Southwest Collection/Special Collections Library, Texas Tech University, Lubbock, Texas. SWCPC D2-11-52-36-1A)

Typical first home of most dirt-poor homesteaders who filed "Four-Section" claims on the South Plains, circa 1900.

Figure 12. Cowchip house

(Courtesy of The Ranching Heritage Center, Lubbock, Texas.)
Cowchips—dried cow manure—were the principal source of heat for A. W. and Mary Blankenship in their treeless South Plains home. But where do you store a winter's worth of cowchips? In 1907, the Blankenships solved that problem by building this cowchip storage house.

Figure 13. The First Courthouse in Lubbock

(Public domain. Courtesy of Southwest Collection/Special Collections Library, Texas Tech University, Lubbock, Texas. SWCPC 57-49-1)

Figure 14. Freighter wagons

(Public domain. Courtesy of Southwest Collection/Special Collections Library, Texas Tech University, Lubbock, Texas. SWCPC D1-1X-18-3)

When the first wave of homesteaders settled on the South Plains near Lubbock in 1902, they had to get supplies from the nearest railroad village, Big Spring, Texas, about 110 miles to the south.

Figure 15. Camp Meeting campsite

(Courtesy of Panhandle-Plains Historical Museum, Research Center. 1984-127/8)

"Revivals" were eagerly anticipated by South Plains settlers. Held each summer during a slack agricultural time (after plowing, planting, tending crops but before harvest time) the meetings were more than a spiritual retreat. For men it was a chance to talk crops, weather, farm animals and to play dominoes. For women it was one of the few times a year when they could escape the drudgery of housework, cooking, and farm chores and enjoy socializing with other women. For children it was a ten-day picnic and games with other kids.

By 1905, the Blankenships had succeeded in drilling their own water well and erecting a windmill tower. By 1907, they had constructed a small outdoor shed in which they stored cow chips for cooking fires and for winter heat. The winter of 1905, their fourth winter, was the coldest. Blizzards swept the prairie, and the Blankenships were running out of food, as well as cow chips and mesquite grubs to fuel their home fire. Coal and food were only available at towns with railroad connections, and the closest was the little town of Big Spring. And to get to Big Spring they had to travel south over an uncharted prairies trail 110 miles. By 1907, the Texas and Pacific Railroad had extended its rails westward past Colorado City on to Big Spring and farther west, but in 1907 Big Spring was the nearest railroad town available to the Strip homesteaders. A round trip wagon journey to Big Spring consumed from eight to fourteen days—unless a snowstorm intervened and obliterated the wagon tracks, then the freight wagons would be delayed. Nevertheless, they decided that to survive Andy would have to make the journey. Mary, with the baby, was left behind to fret and worry. And wait. And hope. And to imagine what disaster might have occurred. Did the team have a runaway? Did the horses get loose from their hobbles during the night? Did a horse step into a prairie dog hole and break its leg? Was Andy hurt? Had he been ambushed? How could she and her baby survive—starving and freezing in that snowbound prison? Mary began climbing the windmill tower each evening to make a lighthouse for Andy by hanging a lighted lantern high in the windmill tower. Finally Andy safely arrived with a wagonload of supplies.[15]

Beside vicissitudes of the weather—blizzards, droughts, and the ever-present danger of wildfires—loneliness and that "fearful solitude" was always there, day after day, year after year. Several years later after more settlers began to stake their claims in the area, that "fearful solitude" was occasionally relieved by community "gettogethers." When the homesteaders organized a few small churches on the South Plains, and during late summer when there was a lull between crop planting and crop harvesting, community camp meetings (revivals) became the social (and religious) highlight of the year. For children it was one big ten-day picnic. For the women it was one of the few times during the year when, freed from the drudgery of housework, farm chores, and tending children, they could relax and enjoy several days of socializing with neighbors and visiting with other women. The community "erupted with life."[16] Some families traveled forty or fifty miles across the plains to attend. Getting ready for a ten-day vacation and preparing food, clothing, water, and supplies and then loading it all in their wagons was no simple or easy task.

Mary Blankenship baked cakes, pies, and bread and cleaned chickens for frying. Clothes were pressed with a flat iron, shoes and boots blacked and maybe half-soled, hair was "home cut," water was carried in and heated for the family baths in the washtub by the kitchen stove, and hair was washed and rolled on stockings or "kid curlers." Up before daybreak, Andy milked the cow while Mary made breakfast and packed. They carried cane-bottom chairs for the women to sit on while riding in the wagon and an umbrella for shade. In addition to the food, they hauled barrels of drinking water for themselves and for the wagon team. Everybody brought their own water. Sacks of feed were included for the horses and mules. Extra bedding—suggans, blankets, quilts, pillows—plus diaper bags, lap robes, tarpaulins, tents, and other items were also loaded. Pots, kettles, ovens, and other kitchen utensils were carried. After all the packing and loading, the home would almost appear deserted. When the morning finally came to hitch up the team "...the excitement felt as though we had been holding our breaths for months."[17]

Chapter 6

Cowmen vs. Plowmen: Tensions Escalate

"I do not believe that the actual settlers have had a fair chance in that country. Mr. Jarrott has reported to me the hardships and trials that home seekers have had contending with the Lake Tomb Co. and other large ranch owners."

Charles Rogan, Commissioner of the Texas General Land Office, Austin, Texas.[1]

April 24, 1902. What happened on that day in Lubbock, Texas, sparked into flame the smoldering hostility that cattlemen had harbored against J. W. Jarrott and his "squatter" clients. April 24, 1902, was the day that J. W. Jarrott and the first group of settlers successfully filed their applications with the Texas General Land Office (GLO) to purchase four-section tracts on the Hockley County portion of the vacant Strip. After the survey, the GLO had classified the strip as "school land," thus making it available for settlers to purchase under the Four-Sections Act.

The cattlemen wasted no time in challenging the GLO's awards to the settlers. The ranchers secured the support of Lubbock County officials including the county judge, county clerk, county tax assessor, the four county commissioners, and the county sheriff, all of whom joined in filing a complaint on May 14, 1902, a complaint that accused Jarrott of unfair practices and demanded that the General Land Office commissioner, Charles Rogan, rescind the awards. Their principal complaint was that the GLO had failed to furnish anyone except Jarrott with a detailed map of the Strip survey prior to taking applications for its purchase. Therefore, without that detailed survey map showing the outer boundary as well as the interior descriptions of each individual section within the Strip lands, it was impossible for the ranchers to apply. The ranchers alleged that:

> ...Not a man on the ground had a map except J. W. Jarrott, and he kept it exclusively to himself...and no map was furnished to the Lubbock County clerk...[2]

The complaint was referred to a state legislative committee for investigation and sworn testimony was taken. Commissioner Rogan responded by pointing out that J. W. Jarrott had personally paid a part of the state-appointed surveyor's fee of $3,000, and therefore he was entitled to a copy of the completed survey. Furthermore, the survey map had been available upon request at the GLO in Austin for more than ten days prior to the filing date and he had given notice of its availability in the state's daily newspapers. In fact, Rogan continued, two South Plains cattlemen, David DeVitt, an owner of the Mallet Ranch, and George L. Beatty, lawyer for the Lake Tomb Ranch, had personally visited his own office during that time and had viewed and discussed the survey map. Moreover, Rogan contended that DeVitt had requested, and had received, a copy of the map.

In the end, the GLO refused to rescind the settlers' four-section awards. In overruling the complaint, Commissioner Rogan expressed his belief that J. W. Jarrott represented "actual settlers" adding that:

> ...The actual settler stands no show out there, with some of the Lubbock County officials and the Lake Tomb people against them...

> and if I can in any way that is right and equitable aid the home-seeker in procuring homes lawfully, I shall do so.[3]

Jarrott's victory in this first showdown with the ranchers may seem to the modern reader to be relatively small. After all, if each of his twenty-five farmer-stockmen clients (including himself) succeeded in establishing a claim to four sections, amounting to only 2,560 acres. What was a mere 2,560 acres when compared to the hundreds of thousands of grassland acres on the South Plains controlled by the cattle kings? At that time, C. C. Slaughter, for example, presided over a huge ranch covering almost 200 sections (128,000 acres), all of which he leased from the state under renewable ten-year leases at a cost of only four cents per acre per year.

In 1896, another cattle baron, M. V. "Pap" Brownfield, had leased 33,250 acres for four cents per acre from the state in the Southeast part of Terry County and established his headquarters on "Lost Draw Creek," located only a few miles from Jarrott's settlers in both Hockley and Terry Counties. And, unlike the absentee owners of the Slaughter ranch and the L7 ranch, "Pap" Brownfield actually lived at the headquarters of his ranch. (See "Where It All Happened" Map in Chapter 8.)

Figure 16. From Cows to Plows

(Public Domain, Courtesy of Southwest Collection/Special Collections Library, Texas Tech University, Lubbock, Texas. SWCPC 460-E2-3)
Bailey County, Texas, farmer pauses while plowing across a cow trail in 1915, as if to symbolize the transformation from cattle raising to farming that was happening on the South Plains of El Llano Estacado.

To the large cattle ranchers on the South Plains, however, the invasion of Jarrott's nesters was viewed with alarm. They feared that if the Jarrott group succeeded it would open the floodgates to hordes of land-hungry plowmen. And that would eventually lead to their fiscal ruin. Hence, they could ill afford to let that camel get his nose under the tent. Viewed from the large operators' perspective, the threat of fiscal collapse was real, and not only from being overrun by four-section homesteaders. Their profit margin also depended on obtaining a cheap long-term lease plus implementing sound management practices. Also, in this semi-arid land cattlemen had to expend large sums drilling, equipping, and maintaining windmills every four miles across their range, as cattle wouldn't graze more than two miles from their source of water.[4] Nature was also a major concern, including threats of a prolonged drought, a freezing blizzard, as well as an out-of-control wildfire. It was also a time when the vicissitudes of the cattle market sometimes triggered disastrous crashes. Hence, these cattlemen's long-range fiscal future hinged on obtaining long-term leases on large blocks of land from the state for pennies per acre and then renewing those leases. They most certainly did not need a swarm of squatters fencing off small tracts in the midst of their pastures as well as running up the cost of state leases—or even worse, forcing them to purchase thousands of acres.

THE FOUR-SECTIONS ACT AND THE LAPSED-LEASE PLOY

After the Civil War, Texas legislators favored railroads, corporations, and large-scale cattle operators. But during the Populist era (1892-1899) the tide turned resulting in, among other legislation, the passage in 1897 of the Four-Sections Act to encourage the settlement of West Texas by farmer-stockmen homesteader families.[5] The Four-Sections Act applied only to tracts classified as "school lands." When, in 1900, GLO land commissioner Charles Rogan became aware of the previously unsurveyed "strip" of land west of Lubbock covering the southern fringe of Hockley and Cochran counties, and the adjoining northern fringe of Terry and Yoakum counties, he classified all the tracts encompassed thereby as "school lands," thus making them subject to settlement by "squatters"—much to the dismay of the large ranch operators. Strip lands came on the market at bargain basement prices: $1 per acre and that payable over forty years.

If the enactment of the Four-Sections Act was a gut punch to the cattle kings, they were soon in for another. This time it was administered by the Texas Supreme Court in an appellate decision declaring a favorite strategy of big operators known as the "lapsed-lease" practice as unlawful. State law provided that at the termination of a lease on state school land, settlers were entitled to an opportunity to purchase (not lease) four section tracts located within the leased acreage. If settlers failed to take advantage of that opportunity then the large cattleman who held the lease on that tract had the right to renew his long-term lease for another extended term. To avoid the risk that some homesteaders might take advantage of the opportunity to purchase a four-section school land tract in the midst of his domain upon termination of his lease, the rancher made sure that his lease never "terminated." This was accomplished by allowing his lease to "lapse" just prior to its termination date by failing to pay the state that last year's lease installment. The lease thus "lapsed," prior to its termination date, but to make sure he never lost possession of any of his ranch land, on the day his lease lapsed the rancher would immediately obtain a new long-term lease from the state covering his entire ranch. One settler challenged that "lapsed-lease" ploy in court, and was successful. In 1902, the Texas Supreme Court in a celebrated case styled *Ketner v. Rogan*[6] declared the "lapsed-lease" trick was an unlawful deprivation of a settler's opportunity to purchase four sections of school land located within the large cattle operator's lease.

"LAND RUSH" BATTLES AT THE COURTHOUSE DOOR

Even after their defeat in *Ketner v. Rogan*, the big ranch operators refused to give up the fight. They did, however, change tactics. Their next challenge focused on the procedure by which settlers filed their applications for the purchase of four-section tracts. Since the price per acre and the terms of the purchase were fixed by law there was no bidding on the land. Instead, applications were accepted only on a first-come-first-served basis at a day specified by the GLO. All applications had to be filed on that date at the county clerk's office in the county where the land offered for sale was located. This procedure proved to have some unforeseen, unfortunate, and sometimes violent consequences. It precipitated what would become known as the era of land rush battles at the back door of the county clerk's office—epic battles to be first in line at 8:00 a.m. on the sale day.

On some occasions when public notice was posted that another parcel of school land would come on the market, cowboy delegates and nester delegates would begin arriving at the clerk's back door sometimes a month or more before the sale date and joust for position in line. Tensions mounted as the sale date approached and threats were exchanged. The local sheriff was obliged to disarm all the contestants upon their arrival and then referee all inevitable threats, fisticuffs, and team brawls. Some county clerks even attempted to maintain order by constructing "chutes" running from outside the courthouses to the clerk's back door. The contestants were required to line up in the chute while attempting to hold their places in line.[7]

J. W. Jarrott's last "land rush" battle to secure four section claims for his settlers occurred on August 23, 1902. The subject school lands were located in Terry County. However, since Terry County was not an organized county in 1902, it had been attached to Martin County, an organized county, the county seat of which was Stanton, a frontier village located approximately 100 miles south of these tracts.

J. W., accompanied by settler G. H. Gist, arrived at the county clerk's office in Stanton several days prior to the sale date and established themselves as first-in-line. There they remained holding the line and sleeping at the clerk's back door. They represented the last thirteen of Jarrott's clients, including, among others, Gist, Noah Bell, and J. W.'s younger brother Ward Jarrott. Soon after their arrival in Stanton, two other eager buyers showed up and got in line behind them: a young lawyer and land agent named D. K. Taylor and another man named Cruz.

Jarrott and Gist continued to hold the line—until one morning when they left to eat breakfast. They placed two substitute line-holders on duty. Unfortunately, the two substitutes were not very vigilant, and when Jarrott and Gist returned from breakfast they discovered that Taylor and Cruz were holding first and second place in line. Fortunately for Jarrott, however, both Taylor and Cruz each filed only one four-section claim for themselves, and not one on behalf of other settlers. That left enough school land available for Jarrott and Gist to file applications on behalf of the last thirteen of Jarrott's contingent.

Claims by thirteen more of Jarrott's four-section squatters came to a total of 33,280 more acres of pasture land to be fenced off and turned under by the plow!

Although there were still hundreds of thousands of acres of grassland available to cattlemen on the Llano Estacado, the ranchers were, nevertheless, worried. Would Jarrott's success touch off an invasion of other poor, land-hungry peasants? Would Jarrott himself (their hero) organize and lead more groups of homesteaders? Even if homesteader claims didn't amount to more than a small fraction of the sprawling Llano Estacado prairie, ranchers and their cowboys resented any intrusion on their turf by what they considered lower class folks—especially sodbusters and sheepherders.

Cowmen intended to see that that never happened again.

During the summer of 1902, while Jarrott was occupied completing the task of securing awards for all twenty-five homesteaders, the cattlemen —one or more of them—concocted another strategy to get rid of these unwelcome squatters. Separate lawsuits were filed against each of Jarrott's Terry County homesteaders. One reason for targeting Terry County homesteaders was that at that time the county was not yet organized, and therefore the law suits had to be filed in the district court in Stanton, and that would require the settler defendants to travel by horse or buggy 100 miles or so to defend their land titles in the Stanton court. And spend considerable time there away from their farms and families while waiting for court procedures to take place.

Unlike previous lawsuits instituted by the big ranchers, these were brought not in the name of the rancher as plaintiff, but rather in the names of individuals who worked for, or were associated with, the ranch owner.

For example, one case was styled *J. W. Barrington v. Noah Bell.* The 1900 Terry County census lists Barrington as a "boarder" on the Lake Tomb ranch. (Less than two years later, J. W. Barrington's name would appear on the docket of another court, this time as a defendant in a criminal case—a murder prosecution.) Another title suit was filed against Jarrott settler J. R. Smith by Bird Rose, the combative and vociferous manager of the Lake Tomb ranch. (Actually, the Chicago syndicate owners of Lake Tomb had also given Bird Rose a small interest in the ranch.) Other Lake Tomb cowboys, Henry Clyborn, Bob Hamilton, and Henry Nightengale also filed individual suits against Jarrott settlers J. E. Woodard, W. H. Gist, and others, including J. W. Jarrott's brother, Ward Jarrott. These lawsuits sought to block approval of the title applications by the GLO on each defendant's four-section tract claim, and also sought damage awards against each defendant. The cowboy plaintiffs contended that the GLO should not approve the settlers' applications because the defendants were not "actual settlers," alleging that they were really "bonus seekers" who sought to purchase four sections of school land for $1 per acre in order to later flip the land to others for a substantial profit. Therefore, the Lake Tomb cowboy plaintiffs contended that Jarrott's "bonus seeking" clients were not entitled under the Four-Sections Act to claim homesteads on state school lands.

On behalf of the settlers J. W. Jarrott filed written answers for each, contending that they were "actual settlers," and countered with the allegation that the cowboy plaintiffs were themselves not "actual settlers," but were in fact simply puppets of a large ranch—namely the Lake Tomb ranch. The first of these individual title suits to be called for trial was *J. W. Barrington v. Noah Bell,* scheduled to begin in the Martin County district court at Stanton on September 16, 1902. Barrington, as well as all the other plaintiffs in these cases were—unsurprisingly—represented by Lubbock attorney George L. Beatty, who represented the Lake Tomb ranch in all its legal matters.

J. W. Jarrott was the attorney of record for Noah Bell and all the other settler defendants. Following his last "land rush" battle on August 23, 1902, J. W. had succeeded in filing four-section applications on behalf of all of his school land clients. Now, beginning on September 16, 1902, he would be obliged to shoulder the burden of appearing in court to defend those titles.

Some person, or persons, plotted to make sure that never happened.

Chapter 7

Death on the Lonely Llano Estacado

"The atmosphere was tense...Lake Tomb and all the other big ranchers had threatened us. I told J. W., 'they're going to kill you... we better get up and get away.' J. W. must have been concerned, but he never showed it."

Mollie Jarrott (later Mollie Jarrott Abernathy)[1]

That summer, the summer of 1902, threats from the South Plains ranchers escalated. They weren't idle threats either. Homesteaders took them seriously. Tensions increased.

Mary Blankenship received word "in a round about way" that the homesteaders had better stop drawing water from ranch windmills.[2] But the use of the ranchers' water was not the real burr under their saddles. True enough, the Blankenships did draw water from the nearest water well located on ranch land. (As noted in the preceding chapter, the ranchers drilled water wells for their cattle about four miles apart.) The ranch windmill the Blankenships used was the only source of water available to them in that sprawling prairie land where no rivers flowed and no lakes were nearby. Just beneath the surface, however, was a huge reservoir of fresh water—the Ogallala Aquifer. The amount of water the Blankenships collected from the ranch windmill was pitifully small, limited to drinking, washing, and household uses, plus watering a couple of horses, compared to the thousands of gallons required each day to quench the thirst of several hundred head of cattle. The Blankenships, like other cash-strapped homesteaders, had to depend on water from the ranchers' water wells until they could scrape up sufficient money to drill their own wells, plus buy and wagon-haul windmills, pipes, and other well equipment for about 110 miles across the prairie from the nearest railhead.

No, water was not the real issue here. Land was the real burr under the ranchers' saddle—an intrusion upon land they considered their domain, their turf.

Somebody sent Mollie Jarrott an unsigned note: "You will take your children and leave the country. You will never hold that piece of land."[3] Another settler, Lee Cowan, brother of Solon Cowan, was threatened at gunpoint while he and two of his sons were inspecting their grain crop. Two cowboys rode up. One pointed a pistol at Cowan saying, "Okay, nester. This is fair warning to you and your kids. Clear off our range. We don't want no sodbusters around. Do you understand?" Lee stood his ground. He stood up straight—all 6'4" of him—and looked the cowboy over. "I'm not leaving. This is my land lawfully. I will not be run off. So you get off my property. If you set foot on it again I will use my rifle to defend it."[4] Shortly after confronting those menacing cowboys Cowan, and other "sodbusters," began noticing that their fence wires were being cut. Lee responded by having his oldest son, ten-year-old Charlie, saddle up each morning, rifle in hand, and check the fence lines. After school he again rode the fence lines before returning home. If he encountered any trouble he was instructed to fire his rifle twice.[5]

Another rancher, Painthorse Hamilton, who claimed Jarrott and his settlers had cheated him out of his range, publicly threatened to kill Jim

Jarrott. He made no effort to conceal his animosity.[6] Another cow man who made no secret of his animosity toward Jarrott was Oliver C. "Bird" Rose, the outspoken and aggressive general manager of the sprawling Lake-Tomb ranch (also known as the "L7" ranch). Not only had the homesteaders intruded on "their" domain by fencing in the unsurveyed (and unleased) Strip land that the L7 ranch had been grazing for free, but also by helping themselves to water from L7 windmills.[7]

One day when Mollie Jarrott was alone out on the Jarrott claim, a rancher she called "old man Combs" rode up. Not realizing who she was, he stopped and struck up a conversation, a conversation that soon degenerated into a rant against that "two-by-four lawyer" Jarrott who was stirring up all the ruckus. Then he asked her this: "What's a woman like you doing out here?" Old man Combs was more than a little abashed when Mollie calmly replied that she was the wife of that "two-by-four lawyer." When he finally recovered, he apologized profusely. And departed.[8]

THE ASSASSINATION

Early in the Month of August 1902:

> Jim and wife, Mollie, walking down the main street of Lubbock, noticing a well-dressed gentleman staring at them from the opposite side of the street. Jim saying to Mollie: "There's a man I'd rather not see in this country."[9]

The gentleman just stood there: motionless, expressionless, silent, all dressed up in a black frock coat, white shirt, and tie, studying Jim Jarrott, fixing him with cold, unblinking blue eyes, making no sign of recognition or greeting. After the Jarrotts passed, the handsome, well-groomed stranger turned and quietly disappeared.

LAST BUGGY TO LUBBOCK

The schoolteacher settler, Florence Watkins, had completed the required annual three-month residency on her claim by August of 1902, and now she had to return to her teaching duties back East at Tarleton College in Stephenville, Texas. Jarrott, who was on his homestead claim that day, volunteered to carry Florence and her baggage back to Lubbock in his two-horse buggy. There she could catch the mail hack from Lubbock to the nearest railroad, that being in Colorado City more than 100 miles south of Lubbock. Jarrott, with Watkins aboard, left fellow settler and ranch hand, John Doyle, at his claim and headed for Lubbock on August 26, 1902. Mollie, meanwhile, was sick and recuperating at the Nicolett Hotel in Lubbock. Their children were also there. After unloading Florence Watkins and her baggage, Jarrott checked on Mollie and spent the night. Next morning he picked up the mail, loaded supplies and left. In his haste to get started, he made a serious mistake. He forgot to take his pistol.

As it turned out, it probably wouldn't have made any difference.

The distance from Lubbock to the Jarrott claim was about thirty miles, a day's trip by horse and buggy, and that meant trotting across Lake-Tomb ranch territory. Approximately three miles northwest of the present-day village of Ropesville, and about twenty-five miles southwest of Lubbock, the ranch owners had drilled two water wells about fifty yards apart, both of which pumped water into a small lake where cattle watered. The pond was located on the prairie between the two windmills. It had been excavated by the ranch with horse-drawn scrapers, and the excavated topsoil had been piled beside the pit. The two windmills were known as "the Twin Towers," also called "the Twin Sisters" and sometimes "the Twin Mills." The Twin Towers pond was the place where Jarrott usually stopped to water his two horses. It was also the place where, in April of that same year, Mary Blankenship had dispatched young Brock Gist to fetch a bucket of water—the assignment that had caused several Lake-

Tomb cowboys to exhibit their hostility by riding ominous circles around the Blankenship claim.

Early Morning, Wednesday, August 27, 1902

The children of Lee Cowan—one of Jim Jarrott's settlers—were playing outside their homestead on the Strip near the present village of Ropesville, then named "Ropes." Sixteen-year-old Grace Cowan later testified that early on the morning of August 27, 1902, she saw a man riding a horse traveling north toward the Twin Mills.[10]

Early Morning, August 27, 1902

The assassin arrived at the Twin Mills site early on the morning of August 27, 1902. He was riding a horse and was armed with a Winchester rifle. Physical evidence later revealed that the assassin had hidden his horse behind the dirt dam made when the pond between the Twin Mills had been excavated. Apparently the assassin had hidden behind one of the windmill towers awaiting his prey, anticipating that Jarrott would, during his return home from Lubbock that hot August day, rein in at the Twin Mills pond to water his horses. The evidence also indicated that he had waited for several hours that hot day before his prey finally arrived at the kill site.[11]

Mid-day, August 27, 1902

When Jim Jarrott, en route from Lubbock back to his claim that day, reined his thirsty team into the Twin Towers pond for a drink, the assassin arose and fired his first round. The startled team swerved sharply to the left away from the pond. Jim Jarrott was wounded but not fatally. When his team served left, he either jumped, or was thrown, to the right toward the pond. The assassin advanced still firing. He fired four, maybe five, rounds. The unarmed Jim Jarrott made it to the pond, leaving a trail of blood. The assassin fired his last two bullets into Jarrott's back while he floundered in the water in a desperate attempt to escape.[12]

The assassin turned and walked away, his assignment completed. He left the dying man in the pond.

J. W. "Jim" Jarrott died at the scene. Forever 41 years old.[13]

Late Afternoon, August 27, 1902

Grace Cowan was still outside her home late that afternoon when she saw the same horseman she had seen that morning ride by. This time, however, he was headed south away from the Twin Towers. She later testified it was the same man riding the same horse she had seen that morning heading north toward the Twin Towers. But she was unable to identify the man.[14]

Figure 17. John Hope in Twin Mills lake

(Author's collection)

John Hope, a contemporary grassroots South Plains historian, stands in the "Twin Mills" lake (long since dried up), located about twenty miles southwest of Lubbock, the site where J. W. Jarrott was assassinated in 1902.

Figure 18. John Hope by Well Casing

(Author's collection.)

Although the two windmills that fed into the Twin Mills lake in 1902 have long since been abandoned and removed, the casing for both still remains cut off about two feet above ground level.

Figure 19. J. W. "Jim" Jarrott

(Public Domain. Courtesy of Southwest Collection/Special Collections Library, Texas Tech University, Lubbock, Texas. SWCPC 326-E 34)
Victim of an assassin's bullet on August 27, 1902, while traveling alone and unarmed on the Llano Estacado twenty miles southwest of Lubbock.

Figure 20. Nicolett Hotel

(Public Domain. Courtesy of Southwest Collection/Special Collections Library, Texas Tech University, Lubbock, Texas. SWCPC D2-6-57-50-1)
The historic Nicolett Hotel was constructed in 1889 in Lubbock. J. W. Jarrott and wife, Mollie, spent their last night together here August 27, 1902.

THE AFTERMATH

There were two routes that settlers customarily took when traveling to and from the Jarrott claim to Lubbock: the northern route and the southern route. The southern route was the one that passed by the Twin Towers. Meanwhile, back at the Jarrott claim Jim Doyle waited, expecting his friend and employer to return on Wednesday, August 27, 1902. Jarrott didn't come. Didn't come the next day. By Friday morning, Doyle, suspecting that something was wrong, saddled up and headed for Lubbock. Settler Griff Hiser rode with him. They took the northern route. Found nothing. Arriving late Friday, Doyle went straight to the Nicolett Hotel where Mollie and the children were staying, Mollie still sick in bed.

Alarmed, Jim Doyle didn't waste words.

"Mother, Jim hasn't come."

She just knew. Knew beyond a doubt.

"They've killed him!"[15]

The search began early Saturday morning. Jim Doyle and pioneer merchant J. D. Caldwell departed Lubbock, this time taking the southern route. Their search ended at the Twin Towers. That's where they found the body, gnawed by scavengers and floating face down in the Twin Towers lake. Jarrott's wagon and both horses were found nearby. Somebody had hobbled both horses, removed the harness and hung it on one of the windmill towers.

They returned to Lubbock with the sad news. Lubbock County Sheriff Barrett Penny was notified; then, to Doyle fell the terrible duty of confirming what Mollie already suspected—knew but had hoped that somehow she was wrong. Ironically, her daughter Elizabeth was at a house party at a Lake-Tomb ranch house near Tahoka. When she regained her composure Mollie sent a friend and a hack to bring Elizabeth home.

Sheriff Penny headed the investigation. They took a sheet with them to wrap J. W.'s body before bringing it back to Lubbock. The investigation was hampered because a heavy rain had fallen on Thursday. Nevertheless, Sheriff Penny made these notes in an attempt to reconstruct the murder:

> A man standing by the tower shot him with a Winchester rifle. This shot seemed to have caused the team to whirl suddenly to the left as shown by the wagon tracks. Blood was found on the right rear wheel and Mr. Jarrott was either thrown or jumped out at the first shot. Traces of blood and tracks were found leading to the lake in which he was found. Two empty shells were found near the water tower and two beside the lake, indicating that at least four shots were fired, and the last and perhaps the fatal one, taking effect in the small of his back. It is believed that Mr. Jarrott ran into the lake and was chased by the assassin...A reward

> of $1,000 has been offered for the arrest and conviction of the assassin or assassins.[16]

Monroe Abernathy, a Lubbock County justice of the peace, also conducted an investigation of the murder scene and viewed the body in the lake. He sketched a complete map of all the surroundings, and on the map he noted that the assassin's horse had been hidden from Jarrott's view because it was staked behind the pile of excavated topsoil that was behind the pond and between the two windmills. The horse had apparently stood hitched at the same place for a long time prior to the killing, this evidenced by the fact that it had stomped a sizeable depression in the ground, indicating that it had been annoyed by flies or other insects during the assassin's vigil.[17]

Mollie, physically ill and emotionally distraught, was unable to get out of bed for her husband's funeral or the burial in the Lubbock Cemetery.

GUN AND BIBLE ON THE FAMILY ALTAR

The reason why J. W. Jarrott was assassinated didn't pose much of a mystery. When direct threats and other unspoken means of intimidation had failed to scare the homesteaders into flight, surely a cold-blooded, calculated assassination of their leader would succeed.[18] Like wildfire, news of Jarrott's assassination swept across the South Plains and beyond. Fear and anxiety invaded every homesteader tent and dugout—particularly among Jarrott's strip settlers. Would they be next on the hit list?

Mary Blankenship later, in her memoirs, recalled that the settlers "expected to be wiped out at any time," that they began carrying weapons wherever they went, and that "our gun and Bible became the family altar as they lay side by side upon the kitchen table."[19]

But the person or persons behind the assassination of Jim Jarrott had badly miscalculated if they thought Mollie Jarrott would retreat or surrender. Mollie: "If those responsible for the murder of my husband thought they would force me to move off the land, they were mistaken, as the only way I would be driven off would be if they buried me beside my husband."[20]

Although Mollie was so sick she couldn't get out of bed to attend her husband's funeral, she rallied and set about shouldering Jim Jarrott's burden. In a horse-drawn buggy she made the rounds of the tents, dugouts and shacks of the homesteaders: "Stay put!" That was her message. Ida Lee Cowan later reflected: "Nothing daunted us. We built a shack and covered it with a wagon sheet...We came with the determination to stay, and we stayed."[21] The settlers bonded in mutual support. Mary Blankenship wrote this: "The name Jim Jarrott became a legend among us, and his martyrdom served to spur us on. We determined not to pull up stakes and retreat back to the East."[22]

THE MYSTERY

Although the answer to the question of why Jim Jarrott had been assassinated seemed obvious, the mystery of who pulled the trigger remained to be solved. Who was the rifleman? And... were others involved in the dastardly and cowardly plot to hide and ambush an unarmed man who had committed no crime?

After considering these questions, there is yet another question that needs to be addressed—one that wouldn't immediately leap to the attention of an investigator. While it is no mystery *when* Jarrott was assassinated, which was August 27, 1902, it is important to consider *why* Jim Jarrott was killed *when* he was killed.

As previously noted, he was scheduled to appear less than three weeks later in the Martin County District Court in Stanton as attorney for five of his homesteader clients, including his brother, Ward Jarrott. In separate "trespass to try title" lawsuits, each client had been challenged to defend the title to his homestead claim. The gist of each of the plaintiff's "trespass to try title" challenge to Jarrott's settler clients was that each client was not really an "actual" bona fide "homestead seeker." While the Lake-Tomb ranch was not the named plaintiff in each suit, it was obvious that the owners of that ranch were the behind-the-scene principals. Lake-Tomb cowboys or others closely associated with the Lake-Tomb ranch were named as the individual plaintiffs in each suit, and Lake-Tomb's lawyer, George Beatty, was the lawyer who had filed each suit and who represented each plaintiff. Moreover, Bird Rose, the fiery manager of Lake-Tomb cattle company (and minority interest owner) filed suit in his own name as plaintiff against settler J. R. Smith seeking not only to defeat Smith's claim to his homestead but also for damages.[23] Other Lake-Tomb cowboy plaintiffs included Henry Clyborn, Bob Hamilton, Henry Nightengale, and J. W. Barrington. Other homesteader defendants represented by Jarrott included J. E. Woodard, G. W. "Ward" Jarrott, W. H. Gist, J. R. Smith, and Noah Bell.

The first case scheduled for trial was that of J. W. Barrington vs. Noah Bell, set to begin on September 16, 1902, in the district court at Stanton.[24] Since J. W. Jarrott was the only lawyer in that South Plains area who championed the homesteaders' interests, if he were killed prior to September 16, then probably there would be no lawyer to take his place when the cases were called for trial. If so then the Lake Tomb cowboy plaintiffs would almost certainly win by default, thus resulting in all the homesteader defendants losing title to their claims. Victory in the court —that and the assassination of the settlers' leader—would surely do the trick and cause the settlers to stampede in retreat. Or so the person or persons responsible for the assassination must have believed.

If so, they again underestimated Mollie Jarrott. Before the trials were called in Stanton in September, Mollie paid a visit to the presiding judge, District Judge William Robert "Will" Smith,[25] who lived in Colorado City. She made sure that Judge Smith understood the situation. And she didn't mince words: "You are [going to be] trying the people who killed my husband."[26]

When the first suit—the one Lake Tomb cowboy J. W. Barrington had filed against homesteader Noah Bell—was called, the court entered judgment for Noah Bell, whereupon all the remaining Lake Tomb cowboy suits collapsed and were dismissed.

The sensational assassination of Jim Jarrott shook the entire South Plains community from center to circumference. It shocked the community—and polarized it. The homesteaders and most town folks were convinced that one or more of the big ranchers had hired an assassin.[27] Most likely within a few days after Jarrott's assassination everyone in the South Plains ranching community had become aware of the identity of the man who was behind the plot, yet publicly the ranchers claimed to be appalled, and soon began circulating rumors that Mollie Jarrott was somehow involved.

Painthorse Hamilton, the rancher who on more than one occasion had publicly threatened to kill Jarrott, was cleared of involvement. At least involvement as the triggerman when it was confirmed that Hamilton was in Portales, New Mexico, the day Jarrott was killed.

Time passed—weeks, months, a year. Whether on account of involvement, complicity or terror, no one stepped forward to point a finger of blame at anyone else.

Mollie: "Nobody didn't try to do a thing."[28]

Except...in the ranching community where those rumors of Mollie's involvement were being circulated. Rumors were even whispered that Mollie was having an affair with Monroe Abernathy, the Lubbock County Justice of Peace, who had been a friend of both J. W. and Mollie.

FINALLY—A GRAND JURY IS CALLED

Whether on account of the rumors of Mollie's supposed involvement or on account of a delayed sense of duty, the district attorney didn't get around to calling a grand jury to investigate the murder of J. W. Jarrott until late in 1903. When J. W. Jarrott's lawyer friends back in Stephenville learned that a grand jury investigation had been slated, the Erath County Bar Association took up a collection and hired one of its own, a skilled trial lawyer named Collin George, to represent Mollie and ensure that the investigation was objective. Collin George arrived in Lubbock, did his own investigation prior to the grand jury hearing, and then told Mollie this: "They're trying to blame you."[29]

The enraged Mollie didn't need a subpoena to appear before the grand jury and testify and didn't attempt to claim any privilege against appearing or testifying. In fact, she demanded a right to be heard and have her say, and when she did she unleashed a blistering tongue-lashing:

> I'm talking right now to people who know who killed my husband! But you haven't got the nerve to do anything about it.[30]

Years later Mollie would recall that tirade, saying that before she was through, all the grand jurors were in tears. "Every man in the room cried. I went through hell." Unfortunately, Mollie could offer no solid evidence as to the identity of the assassin or the identity of any other party who was involved. Lake-Tomb cowboy Ben Glaser did testify and did admit that he had ridden to the Twin Towers scene shortly after the murder at which time he had hobbled Jarrott's horses and hung the harness on one of the two windmill towers. However, he steadfastly denied that he had seen Jarrott's body floating in the lake.

In the end, the grand jury returned murder indictments against four cowboys with connections to the Lake-Tomb Ranch: Ben Glaser, Morgan Bellow, B. F. Nix, and William Barrington—Barrington being the same William Barrington who had filed suit in the summer of 1902, against Noah Bell, one of J. W. Jarrott's settlers, in an unsuccessful attempt to strip Bell of his homestead title. Barrington was indicted for being the triggerman in the Jarrott murder, and the other three were indicted as his accomplices. Glaser was also indicted for perjury.[31]

Mollie never believed that any of these Lake-Tomb underlings were either the triggerman or members of the party or parties who hired the triggerman. Possibly one or more of those four indictees were accessories either before or after the murder, but she didn't believe that any of them were the real villains.

All of the indicted defendants were quickly released on $5,000 bail bonds posted on their behalf by several prominent area men: bondsmen included Frank Wheelock, Van Sanders, W. T. Petty, and M. V. Brownfield. In 1909, Wheelock distinguished himself by becoming the first mayor of Lubbock.[32] Bail bondsmen Van Sanders was a cousin of George Wolffarth, who was the namesake of the misspelled town of Wolfforth located just west of Lubbock. M. V. "Pap" Brownfield executed the bail bond for William Barrington, the alleged triggerman. As this story of the assassination of J. W. Jarrott unreels, it will become apparent that Pap Brownfield played a more important role than merely signing a bail bond.

Because the population of Lubbock County was small and because of the sensational publicity the murder had generated, the district judge on March 17, 1904, entered an order changing the venue of the trials to Floydada in Floyd County, fifty-five miles northeast of Lubbock. And there is where the indictments stalled and eventually died. On May 20, 1905, and September 26, 1905, on a joint motions of the prosecution and the defendants, all indictments were dismissed for lack of evidence.[33]

From there it went into the cold case files. And that's where it remained.

Monroe Abernathy, who was the Lubbock County Justice of the Peace in 1902 when J. W. Jarrott was assassinated and who assisted Lubbock County Sheriff Barrett Penny in the crime scene investigation, had quite an impressive resume. After graduating from Vanderbilt University, he earned a law degree from the University of Texas. In 1898, he served as an officer during the Spanish-American War in both Cuba and the Philippines. Afterwards he served briefly as a state archivist for the State of Texas, and then in 1901, he moved to Lubbock where he was named justice of the peace, an office he held from 1902 until 1905. In 1908 he became a civil engineer employed by the Santa Fe railroad, tasked with the assignment of staking out and securing land titles to its right-of-way when it extended its line from Plainview to Lubbock. Later still, he became a successful investor and land developer in the Lubbock area.[34]

In January 1905, two and a half years after J. W. Jarrott was murdered, Monroe Abernathy and Mollie Wylie Jarrott were married.

Chapter 8

Trail of the Assassin

> "The murder of Jim Jarrott became the South Plains major unsolved mystery."[1]

No one witnessed the execution of Jim Jarrott and, other than a few spent rifle shell casings, the killer left no telltale clues at the crime scene. The crime had all the earmarks of a professional hired gun. But who was he? And who hired him?

No one was ever convicted of—or even tried for—the murder of Jim Jarrott. Years later, a partial answer emerged to at least the first question. Yet more than a century has passed without a definitive solution to that or an even greater puzzle: who hired the killer? And why? And so they remain: the major unsolved mysteries of the South Plains of Llano Estacado.

Now the task begins: fitting together the pieces of the puzzle.

Even though he often—at least when it suited his purpose during his corpse-strewn career—liked to portray himself as a faithful, church-going, God-fearing Christian, the words "bad seed" would have been a more appropriate badge to pin on James Brown Miller's lapel. However, "bad seed" would have been much too kind.

One story has it that when Jim Miller was thirteen years old he murdered both of his maternal grandparents. Then, ten years later, he dispatched his sleeping brother-in-law with a shotgun blast to the head.[2]

THE BEGINNING OF JIM MILLER'S CAREER

James Brown Miller was born on October 25, 1861, in Van Buren, Arkansas, one of the nine children of Jacob and Cynthia Miller. The family history is sketchy, but documents reveal that his family moved to Robertson County, Texas, when Jim was one year old. Later Jim was sent to live with his maternal grandparents in the little village of Evant, Texas, in Coryell County thirty miles west of Gatesville. In 1874, when Jim was thirteen years old, both of his maternal grandparents were murdered in their home, and Jim was arrested for the double slaying but apparently on account of his tender years, he was never prosecuted.[3] It is also documented that after that episode Jim Miller was placed in the custody of his older sister, Georgia. The 1880 federal census verifies that James Brown Miller was living with his elder sister in the Plum Creek community eight miles northwest of Gatesville, and that Georgia was married to a farmer named John Coop. That census also records that Jim Miller's mother, Cynthia Miller, was residing there and notes that she was "widowed or divorced." No record has been discovered to document what happened to Jim Miller's father, Jacob Miller.

Jim didn't get along with brother-in-law John Coop. The headstrong, rebellious, cold-blooded Jim Miller resented John Coop's efforts to discipline him. Finally, Jim had had enough. He devised a clever plan that would put an end to John Coop's provocations by putting an end to John Coop. And get away with murder. On the evening of July 30, 1884, Jim Miller killed John Coop while Coop was peacefully sleeping on the gallery of his home. He never woke up.

Miller had an alibi. Rock solid. Or so he thought. The alibi? At the time of the killing, he was attending a "brush arbor" revival at Camp Branch three miles distant from Coop's home. And he had a very credible witness to corroborate it: he had attended the revival meeting with his girlfriend, Miss Georgia Large. Miss Large did appear as a witness for Jim Miller and echoed his testimony. He had indeed attended the revival meeting with her—had sat by her side. However, on cross-examination, she admitted that although Jim sat "beside her until the preaching began," he had then excused himself and "did not return until the regular service was over and the [inspired congregational] shoutin' commenced." Miller was unable to give an account of his whereabouts during this period of about forty minutes. Time enough, the prosecution demonstrated, for a man to mount up and ride a fast horse to John Coop's house, blow the sleeping man's head off with a shotgun blast, then remount and race back to the Camp Branch meeting and get there "before the shoutin' was over."[4]

The jury found Jim Miller guilty and sentenced him to life in prison, but on appeal the Texas Court of Criminal Appeals overturned the conviction and sent the case back for a retrial. What was the trial court's reversible error? Well, before the trial commenced, Jim Miller had filed motions for a continuance, claiming that he had three more "very credible" alibi witnesses who could testify that he never left the revival meeting the night that Coop was killed, but that he (Miller) needed additional time to locate those three witnesses, subpoena them, and produce them at his trial. The trial court overruled his motions for a continuance and gaveled the trial to order. That, the Texas appellate court held, was a reversible error, and thus Jim Miller was entitled to a retrial.[5] However, by the time the murder conviction against Miller had dragged itself through the Texas appellate process and was finally rescheduled for trial, most of the prosecution's incriminating witnesses had either left the country or "mysteriously disappeared." The prosecution threw in the towel.

The murder of John Coop—its carefully planned execution as well as the resulting trial tactics if a murder indictment resulted—would be a harbinger of things to come in Jim Miller's bloody career. His favored modus operandi: a midnight shotgun blast at close range followed by a speedy exit on a fast horse—spurring hard and deep and being long gone by daylight. But different situations sometimes called for different tactics or weapons: pistols, rifles, or a generous helping of arsenic or nitroglycerine. If arrested the tactics did not vary: obtain a release on bond, hire a good lawyer, then delay, delay, delay. During this time prosecution witnesses tended to "mysteriously disappear" or to suffer a convenient lapse of memory or, if all else failed and the prosecution still insisted on a trial, then Miller would produce a well-rehearsed cadre of flexible defense witnesses: character witnesses, alibi witnesses, or self-defense witnesses depending on the situation.

JOINING THE INFAMOUS MANNIE CLEMENTS OUTLAW FAMILY

After disposing of brother-in-law Coop, Miller drifted to the central Texas area where he fell in with one of the worst outlaw congregations in Texas: the Clements family—the head of which was Emanuel "Mannie" Clements Sr., cousin of the notorious serial killer, John Wesley Hardin. Miller developed a lifelong friendship and collusion with Clements' son, Mannie Jr., and also became enamored with Mannie Jr.'s sister, Sallie, John Wesley Hardin's second cousin. In 1887, the elder Clements became embroiled in a raucous political feud while running for sheriff of Runnels County, the county seat of which is the small north Texas town of Ballinger. During one heated argument, the Ballinger City Marshal, Joe Townsend, shot and killed Clements.

Soon thereafter, while Townsend was riding home one night, a shotgun blast from the darkness blew him off his horse. Townsend survived, but had to have his left arm amputated. The shotgun wielder was never identified, at least not in any official document. But community-wide gossip had it that the triggerman was none other than Jim Miller.[6]

Miller didn't bother to wait around to find out if any indictments fell; he packed up his shotgun and headed west and kept on traveling. Kept on traveling for quite a spell as it turned out and in 1891 ended up in the dry, dusty, and desolate West Texas frontier village of Pecos, the county seat of Reeves County.

Reeves County had been organized in 1883, two years after the Texas and Pacific Railroad had extended its tracks through town on its southwestward journey from Fort Worth to El Paso. Before the railroad arrived, Pecos had consisted of a few saloons, gambling houses, and a café—a remote and untamed speck on the map.

When Jim Miller arrived in 1891, G. A. "Bud" Frazer was the Reeves County sheriff. The Frazer family had been among the first settlers in far West Texas. His father, G. M. Frazer, had been county judge of Pecos County before Reeves County was carved out of its boundaries. Bud was born in Fort Stockton, fifty miles south of Pecos on April 19, 1864. When he was only sixteen years old he joined the Texas Rangers under the command of Captain G. W. Baylor. Later, he served as deputy sheriff of Reeves County, and then in 1890, he was elected sheriff. By 1891, a courthouse, jail, and a church had been constructed and a bank established. Even though law and order had begun to take root, it was still a long way from becoming civilized. One historian described the partially civilized side of town this way:

> Most of the townspeople had settled down to making a living, going to church, having picnics, engaging in a friendly drink now and then, praying three times a day and fist-fighting twice a week.[7]

But that described only the tame side of town. Across the railroad tracks lay "dobie town" (short for "adobe town"), which was a cluster of mud huts where the rough and rowdy crowd hung out, a raw land that "needed a hard-boiled lawmen—someone quick with a gun and not afraid of the devil."[8]

Sheriff Bud Frazer was in dire need of such a deputy.

In August 1891, Jim Miller approached Sheriff Frazer and applied for a job as his deputy, and that's when Bud Frazer made the worst mistake of his life. He pinned a deputy's badge on the most prolific killer and con artist in the state of Texas and did so without bothering to check out Jim Miller's past—neither his background nor his associates. In Sheriff Frazer's defense, however, it should be pointed out that in that day and in that place on the western frontier, a man just never, *ever* asked a stranger where he came from or why he had left there. Dark chapters in a man's past were best left unexplored.

In any event, Jim Miller was now the newly appointed deputy sheriff of Reeves County, Texas. By that fall Jim Miller's best friend, Mannie Clements Jr., showed up with his sister, Sallie, in tow, and Miller took Sallie as his bride. The newlyweds promptly joined the local Methodist church, and when annual revival began in the fall of 1891, deputy sheriff Jim Miller could be found occupying a seat in the "amen corner" at every service. Nobody prayed harder or more fervently than Jim Miller, thus endearing himself to the "good people" of the community.

Soon, however, cattle and horses began disappearing from area ranches. The sheriff sent his deputy out to investigate, but the rustling continued. Deputy Miller spent more and more time away from Pecos, alone, supposedly trailing the thieves to the Mexican border, but he never seemed to be able to catch up with any of them. Meanwhile, more and more livestock kept disappearing.

THE JIM MILLER VS SHERIFF BUD FRAZER FEUD

A western feud of epic proportions soon erupted between Deputy Sheriff Miller and his boss, Sheriff Bud Frazer. It began when Miller killed a Mexican prisoner who Miller claimed was attempting to escape. Frazer's brother-in-law, a crusty old rancher named Barney Riggs, told the sheriff otherwise—said that Miller had been stealing livestock and that the prisoner had incriminating information he was about to reveal

—to wit, the location of two mules Miller had stolen. Frazer promptly went to the location and verified the tip. He found the mules. Then he fired Miller. Instead of making a hasty exit, however, Miller stayed and succeeded in getting himself named the city marshal of Pecos whereupon he hired his outlaw brother-in-law Mannie Clements Jr. as his deputy. In the next sheriff's election Miller ran for sheriff but lost to Frazer.

The feud intensified. Miller next plotted with Clements, M. Q. Hardin, and another sidekick to assassinate Frazer at the local train station when Sheriff Frazer returned from escorting a prisoner to the state penitentiary. The plot failed, however, when one of the sheriff's friends, a man named Con Gibson, got wind of the plan and alerted Frazer. As a result, when the train arrived bringing Frazer back to Pecos he was flanked by the famous Texas Ranger captain John R. Hughes and another ranger. Seeing this, Miller and his associates abandoned their assassination plan and withdrew without firing a shot.

Miller soon discovered that Gibson was the man who had warned Frazer, and in retaliation he dispatched an associate to track Gibson down—found him in the New Mexico Territory and executed him. When Frazer learned about Con Gibson's execution, he was enraged and determined to exact revenge on Miller.

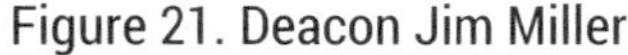

Figure 21. Deacon Jim Miller

(Courtesy of Robert G. McCubbin, Jr.)

A notorious, cold-blooded, remorseless hitman and conman, who once boasted that he had killed fifty-one men "not counting Mexicans." But when he wanted to woo jurors in a murder trial he could also portray himself as a well-mannered, well-dressed gentleman and a faithful church member, hence the nickname "Deacon" Jim Miller.

Figure 22. George A. "Bud" Frazer

(Public domain. Courtesy of Nita Haley Stewart Memorial Library, Midland, Texas. Archives CWW-D9-027 negative.)
George A. "Bud" Frazer (far left) was only twenty-six years old when he was elected as the first sheriff of Reeves County in far West Texas in 1890. Then Frazer made a terrible mistake. He hired Jim Miller as his deputy.

The showdown between Jim Miller and the enraged Bud Frazer took place on the morning of April 12, 1894, on the main street of Pecos. Jim Miller had stepped out of his hotel gallery neatly attired in a suit and black coat. After visiting with a rancher friend, he turned and stared directly into the muzzle of Bud Frazer's six-shooter.

"Miller, you're a thief and a murderer!" Frazer shouted. "Here's one for Con Gibson!"[9]

His first shot hit Miller in the chest. But the bullet seemed not to have any effect. Startled, Frazer fired again as Miller's right hand streaked for his pistol. But Frazer's second shot struck Miller in the right shoulder, disabling his arm. That shot undoubtedly saved the sheriff's life.

Miller, however, reached behind him with his left hand and whipped out his revolver and fired away, but Miller's left-handed shooting was wildly off the mark. Frazer meanwhile emptied his six-shooter, fired three more shots, all hitting Miller in the chest. Frazer then turned and walked away convinced he had put an end to Jim Miller's murderous career.

Some of Miller's friends picked him up and carried him into the hotel and laid him down. Then their jaws dropped in shock! In disbelief! Jim Miller was still alive. When they stripped off his clothing they discovered why. Beneath Miller's coat was a steel plate that protected his chest. An examination of the steel plate revealed that all three of Frazer's bullets had hit within a space of a few inches directly in front of his heart. Miller was still very much alive, but he was seriously wounded from Frazer's shot through his right shoulder. It took Miller several months to recover.

But the Frazer-Miller feud was far from over.

"I'm going to kill Bud Frazer! Kill him if I have to crawl all the way back to Pecos to do it."[10]

The second shootout happened in Pecos on December 26, 1894, with much the same result. Frazer's first shot caught Miller in the right arm. His second bullet tore into Miller's left leg. His third shot again struck Miller in the chest, but again it had no effect. Frazer was still unaware of that steel breastplate. Frazer gaped at Miller. Confused. He knew his aim had been true. It spooked him! Suddenly, he turned and fled.

This time Jim Miller filed an attempt murder charge against Frazer. The case was transferred on a change of venue to nearby Mitchell County, where it was tried. Frazer was acquitted.

The feud was still not over.

Miller was now more determined than ever to kill Frazer. But he wasn't about to challenge Frazer in another face-to-face main street shootout. He crafted a much better, a much safer plan, and patiently waited. Waited for almost two years. Meanwhile, Frazer's term as sheriff of Reeves County expired, and he left office.

On September 14, 1896, Miller received word that Bud Frazer was playing poker in a saloon in the little village of Toyah, just a few miles southwest of Pecos. Miller strolled into the saloon, and without warning took aim at Frazer and emptied both barrels of his shotgun.[11] The double blast of buckshot nearly decapitated Bud Frazer. Then Miller turned and walked away. Proud of his accomplishment, the first thing that Jim Miller did was to drop by the local Western Union Telegraph office in Toyah and send a telegram to his wife. It read:

> Toyah 9/14/1896
>
> TD: Miss Sallie Miller
>
> Bud Frazer and I had a fight.
>
> Frazer is dead.
>
> James Miller

Figure 23. Jim Miller Telegram to Wife: "Bud Frazer is dead."

Form No. 291.
THE WESTERN UNION TELEGRAPH COMPANY.
21,000 OFFICES IN AMERICA. CABLE SERVICE TO ALL THE WORLD.
THOS. T. ECKERT, General Manager. NORVIN GREEN, President.

Receiver's No.	Time Filed	Check
		10 Paid 25c

SEND the following message subject to the terms on back hereof, which are hereby agreed to. Toyah 9/14 1896

To Mrs. Sallie Miller
Pecos
Bud Frazier and I had
a fight [illegible] Frazier is
dead J B Miller

Rn R Y K C
1015 am

READ THE NOTICE AND AGREEMENT ON BACK.

(Public record.)
Miller had feuded with Bud Frazer, former sheriff of Reeves County in far West Texas. Frazer had previously hired him as his deputy. In 1886, Miller caught Frazer unaware (he was playing cards in a saloon) and blasted Frazer with a .12 gauge shotgun. Then he took the occasion to announce his triumph to his wife back in Fort Worth.

Didn't bother to go into any of the gory details. Didn't bother to mention that he'd caught Frazer totally unaware. Didn't claim self-defense. Just proudly proclaimed his conquest of that notorious gunslinger Bud Frazer. The next day, however, he did claim self-defense when he surrendered to the new Reeves County sheriff. Eyewitnesses later identified Miller as Bud Frazer's killer, and Miller was indicted for murder in Reeves County, but Miller and his attorneys realized that a change of venue was of utmost importance for the defense. Bud Frazer had too many devoted friends and family in Reeves County, and too many people were aware of what had really happened in the Toyah saloon when Frazer was decapitated. Self-defense would be a hard hand to play there.

Venue was transferred to the little town of Eastland, which was the county seat of Eastland County and is located 100 miles west of Fort Worth. Eastland was a small, rural county with a population less than 1,000. And, in the late nineteenth century, it had no source of news other than a local weekly newspaper—no daily newspaper, no radio, no television. That being the case, it would make self-defense a much easier sell to an Eastland jury, especially with Jim Miller's well-rehearsed chorus of on-call witnesses waiting in the wings.

The district judge gaveled the trial to order in Eastland on June 3, 1897. The trial proved to be the most sensational event in the history of the tiny frontier town. The hard-fought court battle lasted three weeks. About 150 witnesses showed up, coming from all over Texas. The June 21, 1897, edition of the *Fort Worth Register* newspaper noted that the aggregation consisted of "all the bad men between the Pecos River and El Paso." Tensions peaked. A stampede of lawmen—Texas Rangers, sheriffs, deputies (some of whom were sworn in especially for the anticipated shootout.) The famous pioneer lawman, Dee Harkey, was also summoned to try to hold killings down to a minimum. Lawman Dee Harkey later commented:

> ...there were more bad men testifying for both the state and the defense in that trial than were ever gathered at any one place before. At any rate, I put in twenty one of the damndest days of my life there tending that trial and helping keep order.[12]

It's worth noting that three of Jim Miller's most notorious and well-trained witnesses in the Eastland murder trial were among the nucleus of Miller's congregation of on-call defense witnesses: T. J. Coggin, who sometimes posed as a prominent banker from the small north central Texas village of Merkel; Joe Earp from Coryell County in south central Texas—the county where Jim Miller had previously disposed of his hated brother-in-law, John Coop; and Tom Morrison, who owned a small ranch near Snyder in north central West Texas. In addition to serving as faithful "on-call" witnesses for Jim Miller, all three were also involved in various criminal activities, and all three will have prominent roles to play as this story unwinds.

During the Eastland trial, the prosecution called eyewitnesses who told the jury all about the killing, told how Bud Frazer was concentrating on his poker hand when Miller entered the saloon, how Miller leveled his double-barreled shotgun and blew Frazer's head off. Told that Bud never knew what hit him. Eleven members of the jury voted to convict. But there was one holdout. Apparently gambler Jim Miller went into that game with one ace up his sleeve—just in case all else failed. The judge declared a mistrial.

The case was called for retrial in January 1899, about a year and a half after the first trial. Miller made the most of those eighteen months. Since he was a stranger in Eastland, he devised another defense strategy for the upcoming trial. He depicted himself to the small rural community as being a peaceable, law-abiding, pious, and dedicated Christian—a church-going, non-drinking, non-smoking family man. He and Sallie, together with their two toddlers, visited with most everyone in the sparsely populated county. Never missed Sunday school, or preaching every Sunday evening, or prayer meetings every Wednesday night. Not only that, but Miller accompanied the preacher whenever he made home calls ministering to the spiritual needs of his flock. And so on. That's how he earned the nickname Deacon Jim Miller.

Deacon Jim also took that opportunity to transfer his church membership from his church in Pecos to the local Methodist church, and also to call as character witnesses a number of the faithful members of the Pecos congregation. All agreed that "brother Miller" was a "peaceable man," and one deacon even went so far as to inform the jurors that brother Miller's conduct was as "exemplary as that of a minister of the gospel." During the second Bud Frazer murder trial, it became evident that Deacon Jim's zealous labors in the vineyard of the Lord—or elsewhere—had come to fruition. The jury returned with its verdict: not guilty.[13]

After having barely dodged the judicial bullet, it apparently occurred to Deacon Jim that while revenge was sweet, it wasn't very profitable. Didn't buy a man fancy clothes or diamond stickpins. That in mind, he adopted some new tactics. He persuaded an Eastland saloon owner to sell him half interest in the business. On credit, of course—no money down. Soon thereafter Deacon Jim pretended to leave town for a few days. During his apparent absence, his wife Sallie took a buggy ride with her husband's saloon partner. A pleasant innocent outing. However, when Miller returned, one of his accomplices informed the saloon partner that the Deacon had heard about his buggy ride with Sallie and was threatening to kill him. The terrified partner didn't bother to pack a suitcase. He vanished, never to be heard from again. Miller then sold the saloon for cash, pocketed the proceeds, and left town.[14]

RELOCATING IN THE TEXAS PANHANDLE

After Jim Miller's narrow escape from the jaws of justice in January 1899 during the second Bud Frazer murder trial in Eastland, his first move was to move—move far enough away no doubt to leave his sinister reputation far behind. He chose the frontier village of Memphis, county seat of Hall County, located in the southeast corner of the Texas Panhandle, a land in the rolling plains and low mesa country along the Prairie Dog Town Fork of the Red River.[15] The little town of Memphis might have been only another dot on the map then, but it offered potential for growth and financial opportunities in the near future. Why? Reason was the Fort Worth & Denver City Railroad tracks had recently (1888) been laid through the town—the line running northwest from Fort Worth through the western frontier villages of Wichita Falls, Vernon, Quanah, Childress, and Memphis and continuing on northwest to where Amarillo had just been established, and then on to Denver, Colorado. The railroad caused a population and economic boom to the entire Panhandle. Soon settlers began establishing farms, homes, towns, and stores. The town of Memphis, as Miller undoubtedly anticipated, would become a cattle shipping point for area ranchers to transport their cattle via railroad to eastern markets—no longer would those long, dusty trail drives to Dodge City, Kansas be necessary.[16]

Located twenty miles northeast of Memphis was another village called Wellington, the county seat of Collingsworth County. Soon after alighting in Memphis, Deacon Jim Miller, apparently to gain respectability and create a reputation as an upstanding community pillar and advocate for law and order, succeeded in getting himself appointed as a part time deputy sheriff of Collingsworth County.[17] Not only that, he also succeeded in talking to Collingsworth County Sheriff A. F. Swafford into endorsing his application to be appointed as a Special Ranger attached to Company B of the Frontier Battalion of the Texas Rangers under the command of the famous Captain William J. "Bill" McDonald. The appointment was approved on August 22, 1898.[18] During this time Miller also opened a saloon in Memphis.

SKULLDUGGERY, SECRETS, LIES, AND MURDERS

All went well for Deacon Jim Miller. At least on the surface. For a little while. Yet, all this time skullduggery, secrets, lies, and murders had been going on in the nether world just below the surface. And the pot was bubbling. And Deacon Jim Miller was stirring the mix.

On January 16, 1898, a prominent Collingsworth County rancher named William Janes had been murdered—ambushed and shot dead with a shotgun blast a few miles from his ranch headquarters in the Texas Panhandle. The identity of the killer remained an unsolved mystery, and finally a $10,000 reward was offered by a member of the Janes' family for the arrest and conviction of the villain. Shortly thereafter a man came forward to name the killer (and hopefully collect that $10,000 reward). The volunteer claimed he was an eyewitness to the murder and so testified before the Collingsworth County Grand Jury on November 1, 1898. The grand jury responded by returning murder indictments against the Collingsworth County Tax Assessor-Collector, John R. Beasley, and a cowboy named Will Holmes.[19] The prosecution's key witness, who claimed he was an eyewitness to the murder, was a man named Joe Earp—one of Deacon Jim's on-call witness entourage. What was never explained, or apparently questioned by the grand jury, was what in the world this unemployed drifter, Joe Earp, was doing wandering around an open range ranch pasture in the Texas Panhandle when he just happened to ride up on a murder in progress.

At the time Janes was murdered he was embroiled in a bitter family feud. Although never prosecuted, it was suspected that Janes' son-in-law, L. W. Angel, and Janes' own son, Andy Janes, had killed him. The closeness of the family relationship of the three principals made the possibility of Will Janes' murder by his own son and son-in-law seem incredible, still it was a matter of record that Andy Janes was "often in conflict with the law and that he had a reputation for violence." Also of significance is the fact that a friendship had developed between Deacon Jim Miller, L. W. Angel, and Andy Janes.[20]

To add more skullduggery, secrets, and murder to this scandalous mess, it soon came to the attention of Deacon Jim and L. W. Angel that a man named Jarrett Nelson knew the truth about the identity of the men who had killed William Janes. Nelson knew that John Beasley was an innocent man and that Angel and Andy Janes were the killers, and that Deacon Jim Miller was the man behind the plot. They also became aware that Jarrett Nelson was about to appear before the Collingsworth County grand jury. But he never made it. He was ambushed and murdered en route to Wellington.[21] Meanwhile, Miller's plot to collect the $10,000 reward for the arrest and conviction of John Beasley for the murder of William Janes was about to become unraveled.

To collect that $10,000, Beasley had to be convicted, and the time was drawing near for Beasley's trial. Venue had been changed from Wellington to the small town of Vernon ninety miles southeast of Wellington. John Beasley continued to stoutly deny that he had any involvement in the murder of William Janes. Yet, the prosecution had an eyewitness to the murder—a man named Joe Earp—who was going to testify that John Beasley was the assassin.

Then the face of fate smiled down on John Beasley.

A purely coincidental conversation during a train ride blew the prosecutor's case out of the water. That's when Beasley's defense lawyer happened to meet Dee Harkey, who happened to remark that he had served as a special deputy, charged with keeping the peace during Miller's trial in Eastland. During further conversation the defense attorney also learned that Dee Harkey knew Joe Earp, and that Earp had been one of Miller's chief defense witnesses in the Eastland trial. That's when Beasley's defense lawyer's ears really perked up. Furthermore, it turned out that Harkey had seen Joe Earp in Eastland on the very day that Earp had sworn to the Collingsworth County grand jury that he had witnessed Beasley murder the prominent stockman William Janes on his ranch, approximately 200 miles northwest of Eastland.

When Harkey learned that Joe Earp was slated to testify that he had witnessed the William Janes' murder, Harkey agreed to accompany Beasley's defense lawyer to Vernon and confront Earp. Just before the trial was to begin, Beasley's defense attorney, together with Dee Harkey and the prosecuting district attorney J. M. Stanlee, confronted Joe Earp. That's when Earp realized that the blade of a perjury conviction was now poised menacingly just above his neck, and that's when Earp quickly recanted his prior grand jury testimony and admitted that Beasley was innocent, adding that Miller had "fixed the frame" in order to collect the $10,000 reward.[22] Earp added that Miller had offered him $75 for playing his role as the prosecution's star witness as soon as he collected the $10,000 reward, although he did generously advance Earp $25. Earp also disclosed other statements made by Miller that confirmed Miller's involvement in Janes' murder. According to Earp, Miller even pointed out the exact spot out on the range where Janes had been assassinated.

The murder indictment against Beasley was promptly dismissed, replaced by a subornation of perjury indictment against Deacon Jim Miller (for inducing Joe Earp to lie to the grand jury when he testified under oath that he had witnessed John Beasley kill William Janes). The case was moved from Vernon to the nearby town of Quanah in Hardeman County where it was tried on October 3, 1901. District attorney J. M. Stanlee, vigorously prosecuted the case and persuaded the jury to find Miller guilty and assess his punishment at five years in prison. The state's key witness was turncoat Joe Earp. (Although Miller lost that jury trial, two of the usual cadre of Jim Miller's defense witnesses who showed up for his trial are worth pausing to note here: T. J. Coggin and Tom Morrison. Much more about those two renegades lies ahead as our story unfolds.)

Deacon Jim Miller appealed his conviction, and on December 31, 1901, the appellate court not only reversed the trial court conviction of Miller for subordination of perjury, but it also dismissed the underlying indictment thus making a retrial of the case impossible—dismissed the indictment because it had been returned by the grand jury after the statute of limitations on that offense (subordination of perjury) had expired.[23] Thus, once again the Texas Court of Criminal Appeals rescued Deacon Jim Miller from a long stay in prison—just as it had done fifteen years earlier when it had relieved him from doing a life sentence for murdering his brother-in-law John Coop.

Without a doubt Joe Earp breathed a deep sigh of relief when he dodged a stretch in the Texas pen for perjury by recanting his lie implicating Beasley in the murder of William Janes. He had indeed accomplished that, but by so doing he should have realized that he had just jumped out of the proverbial frying pan directly into the fire. Insofar as Deacon Jim Miller was concerned, Joe Earp had just committed an unpardonable crime. One that called for a death sentence. One that no appellate court could reverse. And the taste of revenge would be sweet.

The day the jailhouse door was opened by the appellate court in 1901, Deacon Jim Miller hit the ground running, openly bragging this:

> Joe Earp turned state's evidence on me, and no man can do that and live. Catch the papers, boys, and you'll see where Joe Earp died.[24]

Sure enough, three weeks later Earp was ambushed and killed near Gatesville in Coryell County, which is approximately 350 miles southeast of Collingsworth County in the Texas Panhandle where William Janes was ambushed and murdered. No one was ever arrested for the murder of Joe Earp. Deacon Jim Miller later boasted to Charles R. Brice—a lawyer living in Memphis, Texas, who later moved to New Mexico where he served as chief justice of the New Mexico Supreme Court—that he made sure he would never be convicted of Earp's murder, explaining "I rode a hundred miles that night and sent a telegram to establish an alibi."[25]

Joe Earp had paid the price for crossing Miller, but circumstantial evidence also leads to the conclusion that Miller's taste for revenge was still not sated. He nurtured a grudge against District Attorney Stanlee for denouncing him so fervently and so vigorously before the jury so that it was persuaded to convict him of subordination of perjury.

Not long after Joe Earp paid the price for betraying Miller, District Attorney Stanlee died under very suspicious circumstances. Although Stanlee lived in Vernon, his multi-county district court docket often took him to Memphis, Texas, where in the fall of 1901, he spent the night in the local hotel. The hotel served supper each evening to its guests, and Stanlee ate supper there. During the night he became ill, deathly ill, and the next morning he died. A doctor examined his body and entered "peritonitis" as the cause of death.

Much later the doctor confided to a brother of Judge Brice that the real cause of Stanlee's death was not peritonitis, but arsenic poisoning. The doctor admitted that his initial diagnosis was erroneous, that he had intentionally misdiagnosed the cause of death because he had been afraid to document arsenic as the actual cause of death—afraid of retaliation by Jim Miller. The doctor added this: he had conducted a secret investigation of his own and discovered that the regular hotel cook had not been on duty the night the district attorney became ill soon after eating his supper. A substitute cook, a friend of Jim Miller's, had replaced him. Then, the next day—the day that Stanlee died—the substitute cook disappeared, and was never heard from again.[26]

GUN FOR HIRE: CASH UP FRONT

At the turn of the century, Deacon Jim moved to Fort Worth and bought a downtown rooming house, the day-to-day management duties of which he assigned to his wife, Sallie. He had more important matters to attend to. Hanging out at lobbies of the best hotels and at gambling tables in the best saloons, he socialized with prospects. His reputation as a hired gun had preceded him. No target was immune. Cash up front, no questions asked.

In that era some of the big cattle operators in West Texas began to become annoyed by the encroachment of sheepherders and sodbusters who were settling on "their" turf. Meantime, over in the outlaw-infested Oklahoma and Indian Territories, ongoing battles raged between lawmen and outlaws as well as bitter feuds between families, between neighboring landowners and between other factions—feuds that often simmered, erupted, and turned deadly. Consequently, in both venues there was a market for Miller's skills. During the next several years Miller drifted in and out of his home base in Fort Worth on his deadly missions, sometimes being gone for several weeks. His going rate for disposing of sheepherders was reportedly $150 per victim, later bragging that he had killed eleven or more Mexicans—hadn't bothered to keep count.

Although a firearm, whether a rifle, a pistol, or his preferred weapon, a shotgun, was Deacon Jim's usual instrument of extermination, it was not, as we have learned, his only weapon—recall District Attorney Stanlee's arsenic supper. One West Texas rancher was infuriated when a sheepherder filed a homestead claim on four sections in Nolan County, Texas, near the town of Sweetwater and had then promptly populated it with about 2,500 head of sheep. The rancher was determined to terminate his problem. He contacted Jim Miller in Fort Worth.

The next day, Miller showed up at the Renfro Drug Store owned by the prominent Fort Worth druggist, E. T. Renfro. Miller said he had an old worn-out stallion that "needed to be put down." Renfro advised spiking his horse feed with nitroglycerin. Miller bought a dose large enough to kill a horse, leaving however with a warning from Renfro to handle it with care: "That stuff can explode on you."

Apparently, the Deacon heeded the druggist's advice and handled the prescription carefully—very carefully—carrying it by horseback for 125 miles to the sheepherder's camp out in Nolan County. Got there just before supper time, greeted the herder with his usual charm and good cheer, and was invited to stay for a meal. To return his host's hospitality Miller suggested that they have a toddy, then produced a whiskey bottle —and poured his host a drink.

Next day the coroner ruled it "death by heart failure."

A few days later the deacon was back in Fort Worth and encountered Renfro on the street.

"How'd the nitro work for you?"

"It surely does work."

Years later, Renfro would reflect that from further conversation with Miller that day, and from what he had subsequently learned about Miller's adventures he became convinced that it was the sheepherder, not the stallion, who had enjoyed the deacon's before-supper toddy.[27]

Farther West along the Pecos River, in about 1900, a cattle baron kept losing calves and suspected that two known rustlers were the cause. Miller was hired to solve the problem. When he arrived at the ranch headquarters, he requested a horse, a bedroll, supplies, and rations for a few days. Then Miller mounted up and rode away. Several days later he reappeared, returned the rancher's horse to his corral, and announced that he had completed his assignment. Reassured the cowman that he wouldn't be losing any more calves. Cowboys later found one of the rustlers lying dead on the prairie near the Pecos River, shot once in the head. They also found two saddled, riderless horses roaming nearby. But no second body.

Bill Carter, one of the ranch cowhands who found the two horses and the corpse, puzzled over what had happened to the second rustler. Later when Carter took some of his employer's cattle to market in Fort Worth he happened to run into Deacon Jim Miller and asked him about the missing rustler. He got this explanation: Miller said he hid and waited for two days near the Pecos River before the rustlers appeared. He shot one in the back, but the other rustler made a mad dash to escape and nearly got away, but finally when he got to the Pecos River he jumped off his horse and attempted to wade across. That's when he got hopelessly mired in quicksand. And that's where Miller left him. Didn't have to waste a bullet on him. Just watched him slowly sink and then disappear.[28]

At this point in his career, Miller's fee for relieving big operators of Mexican sheepherders was $150 per intruder, but for Anglo rustlers and for nesters it was now $500 per hit. He later boasted that $500 was what he had charged to get rid of one of those troublesome Anglo nesters on the South Plains near Lubbock—as we shall soon learn.

HITMAN AND CONMAN

By 1904, it became apparent that Deacon Jim Miller, having polished his consummate skills as a slick con artist as well as a sure-shot hired gun, was enjoying life on a grand scale in Fort Worth. He decked himself out in expensive, finely tailored new clothes including a stylish black coat, and a brand new Stetson hat, sported an impressive diamond ring on his finger and an expensive diamond stick pin on his shirt collar. All that fancy rigging combined with Gentleman Jim's high-toned manners, good looks, calm demeanor, smooth talk, and self-assured style, well...

he just looked for all the world like a highly successful and legitimate businessman. (As early as 1901, the Fort Worth city directory listed James B. Miller's address as 309 Rusk Street and his occupation as "Real Estate Agent.") Plus, of course, to the general public in Fort Worth Deacon Jim Miller continued to portray himself as a wholesome family man and a dedicated church member.

Meanwhile, his land scams became more sophisticated. To facilitate his scams Miller stole an official State of Texas Notary Public seal, which he employed to lend the appearance of authenticity to the signatures of parties to forged land transaction documents. Deacon Jim pulled off one of the smoothest land scams of his career. Without a dime down he acquired sole ownership of the Old Exchange livery stable in Fort Worth, including all its horses, buggies, wagons, and good will—all that in exchange for Miller's notarized deed conveying to the stable owner five sections of land (3,200 acres) located on the Gulf Coast in Matagorda County about half way between Galveston and Corpus Christi. The livery stable owner, who was described as "a young man of great strength and sort of a bully" was mighty proud of his land acquisition and who couldn't wait to get down to the gulf and explore his new rancho grande, mounted his horse, stuffed Miller's deed in his saddlebag, and off he went. When he arrived and proudly displayed his deed to Matagorda County's official land surveyor, the surveyor took one look at the land description, shook his head, and informed the former stable owner that his rancho grande was located about two miles out in the Gulf of Mexico.

Miller soon heard that this latest sucker, the former livery stable owner, was enraged and stalking him. That's why he checked to make sure that his pistol was loaded and then took the extra precaution of hiring two bodyguards. He was astonished, however, when the confrontation occurred. His victim approached him "in a friendly manner," and said, "You sure cleaned me out, but now I want you to help me sell my [Matagorda] ranch." Then he named a fellow who had bested him in a previous transaction and who had "lots of money." Miller and his most recent victim then joined forces, left Fort Worth, found the new target, whereupon Miller once again sold the Matagorda "sea ranch." He and the previous livery stable owner returned to Fort Worth with a bundle of cash.[29]

THE FRANK FORE MURDER

The deacon's next land swindle didn't have such a pleasant or non-violent ending. In its March 10, 1904, edition, the *Fort Worth Star-Telegram* reported that Jim Miller "has had much to do with buying and selling lands." The article then continued informing its readers that Miller and several associates were under investigation for forgery of land titles and securing fraudulent loans. The scam played out like this: Miller and associates appeared to have obtained an absolute and unencumbered title to "the Burford farm." Problem was, however, title to the farm had been acquired by virtue of a forged deed. Miller and friends then pledged the bogus land title to the Burford farm as security for a $16,000 mortgage loan obtained from the American Freehold Land and Mortgage Company in Fort Worth. Deacon Jim, of course, defaulted when the note came due. The mortgage company then attempted to foreclose its lien and that's when it discovered the fraud. The mortgage company hired a former deputy US marshal from the Indian Territory named Frank Fore to conduct an investigation. Fore's investigation resulted in forged land title indictments being returned in the Fort Worth district court against Jim Miller and five others, including Miller's close friend, a livestock trader named Berry B. Burrell—a man soon destined to become much closer to Deacon Jim Miller. In life and in death.

Frank Fore was a tough and rough-hewn character from Oklahoma's wild Indian Territory, previously employed as a US deputy marshal in 1898 and had worked under the authority of federal court in Paris, Texas, and in the Indian Territory court in Ardmore, before retiring in 1902. During his time as a deputy marshal he had faced some desperate characters, and had been engaged in a score of shooting scrapes in

Denison, Paris, and other north Texas towns as well as in the Indian Territory. Although Fort Worth folks regarded Frank Fore, now age 50, as a fearless "rough customer" who could "hold his own in a scrimmage." He was generally well liked in Cowtown. (Fort Worth's nickname.)

March 10, 1904. That was the date of the fatal confrontation between Jim Miller and Frank Fore. It happened in the lavatory of the Delaware Hotel in Fort Worth. Two shots were fired. When the smoke cleared Frank Fore lay dying, face down on the floor, a .45 caliber pistol wound in his left chest, and another wound in his left hand. An unfired pistol was found beneath Fore's body. Jim Miller exited the restroom, calmly strolled down the street to the Tarrant County sheriff's office and surrendered, announced to the startled officers that he had just shot and killed Frank Fore... in self-defense of course, and told them where to find the body.

Tarrant County attorney O. S. Lattimore was notified and hurried to the scene and found Fore where he had fallen. But Fore wasn't dead. The mortally wounded Fore made a dying declaration to the county attorney—said that Jim Miller had ambushed him without warning. Denied making any threat or any attempt to pull a pistol on Miller. Frank Fore lingered for two days before dying.

Meanwhile bond was set for Miller at $2,000. It was promptly posted by two of Miller's cronies (one of whom was T. J. Coggin), and the deacon was turned loose to resume his career. The trial was postponed for more than two years; Miller, running true to form, stalled the proceedings with numerous motions for continuances by alleging that he was having difficulty locating various important defense witnesses.

When the trial finally got underway it appeared to be an easy downhill ride for the prosecution. Premeditated murder in the first degree; no question that Miller had killed Fore; no wiggle room there for a mistaken identity or an alibi defense. That left self-defense as the only possibility. But what possible motive would Frank Fore have had to kill Miller? None apparent. Deacon Jim on the other hand had plenty of motive to silence Fore, since Fore was on tap to be the star prosecution witness when

Miller's trial on the forged land deed and bogus loan transaction cases were called. Ironically, Frank Fore, though now deceased, would also be the prosecution's linchpin witness waiting in the wings to fit that noose around Miller's neck. Even though Frank Fore's dying declaration made to County Attorney Lattimore was hearsay evidence, it was nevertheless admissible under an exception to the Texas Rules of Evidence. The underlying rationale for this being that a man who is dying, and realizes that he is dying, and is not likely to go to his grave with a lie on his lips. Therefore, County Attorney Lattimore was permitted to inform the jury that according to Frank Fore's account of the incident, Jim Miller had ambushed him in the lavatory without warning, shot him twice, and left him for dead. In his dying declaration Frank Fore didn't mention anyone, except himself and Miller, being inside the lavatory when the shots were fired.

But the murder trial would not be a quick and easy romp for prosecutors. Undeterred by all the incriminating evidence in the prosecution's arsenal, Miller subpoenaed his usual retinue of defense witnesses—witnesses who hailed from towns and villages all across the sprawling state of Texas. About 100 witnesses were rounded up, two-thirds of whom were defense witnesses. Peculiar it was—mighty peculiar—that nearly all of Miller's defense witnesses lived a far piece away from Fort Worth, yet they just happened to have been congregated in Fort Worth on the day of the shooting—a number of whom also just happened to have been in or around the Delaware Hotel when the shots were fired. The defense attempted to explain their presence by pointing out that the Texas Cattle Raisers Association was having its annual meeting in Fort Worth at the time. Still, that left a large number of defense witnesses who had little, if anything, to do with the cattle business, except maybe rustling a few critters now and again—witnesses such as Miller's brother-in-law, outlaw Mannie Clements, and his friend, M. Q. Hardin, the pair who had plotted with Miller to ambush and kill the Pecos sheriff, Bud Frazer, a decade earlier. Another Miller witness was J. N. Webb, the outlaw sheriff of Dallam County in the Texas Panhandle who at the time was under indictment for murder and who would later be indicted for his involvement in an illegal Chinese immigrant smuggling operation headquartered in El Paso. And, of course, Miller regulars, T. J. Coggin and Tom Morrison, also "just happened" to have been on the scene and so were subpoenaed to testify for the defense.

When Miller exited the lavatory after he shot Fore, he apparently assumed that Fore was dead, or soon would be. But then he learned that Fore had survived long enough to make that very incriminating "dying declaration" to the county attorney: one that would be quoted to the jury, one that would deny Miller any credible basis for a self-defense plea, and one that would also verify that only he (Fore) and Miller were present in the lavatory when Miller shot him.

That's when Miller was painfully reminded of that old shopworn saw: "The best-laid plans of mice and men..." And that's when he realized that he was in serious—very serious—need of a powerful eyewitness to the shooting, one who would effectively rebut Fore's assertions. And that's when Deacon Jim executed and presented to the court a sworn affidavit attached to his request for a subpoena for the appearance of such a key defense witness.

Surprisingly enough, that key eyewitness turned out to be a newcomer to Miller's usual team of defense witnesses, one who would prove to be both a very believable and a very persuasive witness—a star on the stand —a Terry County cattle baron by the name of M. V. "Pap" Brownfield.

The Frank Fore murder trial, when finally called, lasted two months during which Miller paraded his well-rehearsed battery of defense witnesses to the stand. Finally, on May 4, 1906, the jury returned a verdict of "not guilty." It had taken the jury only fifteen minutes of deliberation to arrive at that conclusion.[30] That being the case, the American Freehold Land and Mortgage Company was forced to dismiss the forged deed swindling indictments against Miller and associates. Thus Deacon Jim departed the Fort Worth courthouse that day a free—and much wealthier —man.

THE ASSASSINATION OF US DEPUTY MARSHAL BEN COLLINS

August 1, 1906. Less than three months after the Fort Worth jury acquitted Deacon Jim in the Frank Fore murder trial, a coroner in the Indian Territory of Oklahoma pronounced US Deputy Marshal Ben Collins dead, killed near Tishomingo by two shotgun blasts during a nighttime ambush. The Chickasaw Indian Territory National Counsel offered a $1,000 reward for the arrest and conviction of the killer. Ben Collins' family hired a private detective to work with law enforcement officers. Eventually evidence was amassed that led to the indictment of Deacon Jim Miller and two accomplices. The evidence further revealed that Collins' murder had resulted from a bitter, bone-deep grudge held by the family of Port Pruitt, a prominent citizen of the little town of Orr, Indian Territory, and his brother Clint Pruitt, a well-to-do citizen of the nearby town of Cornish. In a previous confrontation Marshal Collins had, in 1903, seriously wounded Port Pruitt and paralysis had been a result. Brother Clint was determined to avenge his brother's disastrous confrontation with Collins, but he lacked the nerve to call him out. So he hired a proven assassin to do the dirty work, and paid Deacon Jim Miller $1,800.

A posse led by veteran lawman US Marshal John A. "Jack" Abernathy and assisted by Deputy US Marshal Frank Canton and local officers, set out to locate and arrest the assassin. Jim Miller was eventually trailed to his sister's home near Hobart where he had been hiding. The lawmen quietly surrounded the house. Miller, aware that Abernathy was determined to take him—dead or alive—quietly emerged from his sister's home, hands up, and surrendered. Miller shrugged it off, casually remarking, "I've got out of other scrapes, and I reckon I will this one."[31]

Figure 24. US Marshal John R. "Catch 'em-Alive" Jack Abernathy

(Public domain. Reproduced from *"Catch 'em Alive Jack:" The Life and Adventures of an American Pioneer* by John R. Abernathy by permission of the University of Nebraska Press. Copyright 1936 by the General Board of the Young Men's Christian Association.)

The rawhide tough U.S. Marshal in the Oklahoma Territory was the cousin of Monroe Abernathy of Lubbock, Texas, who married Mollie Jarrott after her husband Jim Jarrott was assassinated. In 1906, U.S. Marshal Abernathy arrested Deacon Jim Miller for the Oklahoma Territory murder of Deputy U.S. Marshal Ben Collins, and in a friendly chat with Marshal Abernathy, Miller casually confided that he had assassinated J. W. Jarrott back in Texas in 1902.

Deacon Jim Miller had good cause to surrender peaceably to US Marshal Jack Abernathy, the rawhide tough, fearless and feared Oklahoma Territory lawman, who, in addition to his reputation as a professional outlaw hunter, had gained fame for his Wild West-style wolf hunting expertise. Mounted on a fast steed, once Jack spotted a wild wolf, he spurred hard and deep and gave chase across the Oklahoma prairie until he overtook the tiring beast and then bailed off his horse and bulldogged the critter. Then, with his bare hands, Jack would clamp the animal's jaws together and wire them shut. Hence, his nickname "Catch 'em-Alive Jack" Abernathy. (Later, after he retired, he wrote and published a book, using his nickname in the title.)[32] Marshal Jack Abernathy also gained fame in 1905—the year before he arrested Deacon Jim Miller—when he demonstrated his Wild West wolf catching skill for US president Teddy Roosevelt, who was himself famous for his outdoor adventures. In addition to President Roosevelt, others witnessing Marshal Abernathy's wolf-chasing skill that day in 1905 were several Oklahoma and Texas cattlemen including, among others, Guy Waggoner and S. B. "Burk" Burnett, plus famous Texas Ranger captain Bill McDonald and Comanche Indian chief Quanah Parker.

The following year, August 1906, when Marshal Abernathy arrested Deacon Jim Miller for the murder of Deputy US Marshal Ben Collins, "Catch 'em-Alive Jack" told Miller that since he had surrendered peaceably he would not bother to lock handcuffs on his wrists or leg irons on his ankles during their lengthy train ride to the Guthrie jail. The prisoner expressed his appreciation and promised Abernathy he would give him no trouble. Warming to the relationship, Miller became talkative on their journey, boasting that he had been tried in courts for murder about fifteen times and was always able to be cleared by calling witnesses to support his self-defense or alibi claims. He related how he had beaten the murder charge for killing ex-sheriff Bud Frazer during the Eastland trial. At that point Abernathy asked him how many other killings he had gotten away with—murders that hadn't resulted in trials. That's when Miller claimed the total to date was fifty-one men—not including

Mexicans. That's when he added the comment about having "lost his notch stick on Mexicans." When Marshal Abernathy pressed him for details of these unindicted murders, Miller refused to elaborate, saying, "I'm not on the stand." However, when Abernathy assured him that any incriminating admissions would be completely off the record and that he wouldn't use any disclosures against him, Miller opened up and bragged about some of those "notches" he'd gotten away with without having to win a murder trial.

One of the next questions Abernathy asked was, "Who was the hardest man to kill in your experience?"[33]

Miller's answer to that one, if believed, would clear up an unsolved murder mystery. But the marshal abided by his pledge of confidentiality and kept Miller's disclosure secret. That is, he kept that pledge for as long as Miller lived, revealing it only a quarter of a century after Miller's death. And, as we shall soon discover, what a blockbuster of a disclosure it proved to be.

Marshal Abernathy delivered his prisoner to the jail in Guthrie on December 6, 1906. The next day's edition of the *Oklahoma State Capital* took the opportunity to print a lead article on "gentleman" Jim Miller, informing its readers that he was a "Texas outlaw who has escaped several courts." Then added this: "He is a peculiar character and boasts that he never gives up to an officer unless he first gets 'the consent of his own mind.' He is also peculiar in his habits. He neither chews, smokes or drinks whiskey."

Eventually the murder trial of Miller for the ambush assassination of Deputy Marshal Ben Collins was continued, postponed, and delayed until finally the indictment was dismissed. Time does indeed have a way of thinning out the prosecution's witness list in a cold case file—whether by death, distance, or persuasion. James B. Miller had once again dodged another hangman's noose.[34] Meanwhile, upon his release he departed Tishomingo and headed back to Fort Worth where he received word that another prospective customer was waiting to engage his services.

THE ASSASSINATION OF PAT GARRETT

The next summons for Miller's service came from New Mexico, and it would involve Deacon Jim Miller in one of the most—if not *the* most—sensational assassinations in the history of the Old West. The target: famed and feared New Mexico lawman Pat Garrett.

It had been twenty-seven years since Pat Garrett made headlines across the Southwest when he killed the famous frontier outlaw Billy the Kid. Afterward, he served as sheriff of Dona Ana County, New Mexico Territory, county seat of which is Las Cruces, and then later as the federal customs collector at El Paso before retiring to his ranch in the Organ Mountains east of Las Cruces. During his long career as a lawman in the outlaw-infested New Mexico Territory, Pat Garrett had made many friends. But he also had made many enemies, some of whom were influential—and embittered. But none quite brave enough to take on Pat Garrett, the famous manhunter of Billy the Kid, in a face-to-face confrontation. Ergo the call for Deacon Jim Miller's services.

Jim Miller, himself an in-law of the infamous Mannen Clements family of outlaws, was to meet another Clements family in-law outlaw: Carl Adamson. Adamson was not only an in-law of the family, he was also a kindred spirit, actively engaged in sheep and cattle rustling and various fraudulent schemes including the smuggling of illegal Chinese immigrants into the United States, crossing the border at El Paso. Now he contemplated adding the crime of murder to his resume.

Pat Garrett was assassinated on February 28, 1908, on a lonely stretch of road near Las Cruces in Dona Anna County, New Mexico. Who killed Pat Garrett? Was it Jim Miller? Or someone else? The sensational story has triggered speculation for more than a century and has been explored in many books and articles.[35]

Captain Fred Fornoff, chief of the New Mexico Mounted Police, contended that sometime in mid-February 1908, Jim Miller met with a "wealthy rancher" in a lawyer's office in El Paso who paid Miller $1500 to kill Pat Garrett. A part of the bargain was that the rancher was to furnish a "patsy" who would confess and take the blame for the killing as well as an "eyewitness" to corroborate the patsy's claim of self-defense.[36]

Accordingly, Miller concocted a plot to do the deed. He and Adamson would pose as cattlemen who had just purchased 1,000 head of cattle in Old Mexico and needed to bring them across the border and find a pasture home for the critters through the coming summer until they could be shipped next fall to Miller's (non-existent) ranch in Oklahoma. They would approach Pat Garrett and offer him a lucrative contract to pasture the cattle on his ranch. When approached, Garrett (who was in dire financial straits at the time) was eager to close the deal as soon as possible.

On February 28, 1908, Adamson arrived at Garrett's ranch in the Organ Mountains on the pretext of wanting to pasture the Mexican cattle there. Next morning Carl Adamson and Garrett set out for Las Cruces in a two-horse buggy. Along the way they encountered Wayne Brazel, a dull-witted cowboy who had been running some goats on Garrett's ranch. Brazel rode his horse alongside Garrett's buggy. About five miles east of Las Cruces, Adamson reigned the horses to a halt. He and Garrett got out of the buggy.

Shortly before noon that day, Dona Ana County Deputy Sheriff Felipe Lucero was sitting in his office in Las Cruces when a distraught Wayne Brazel burst in and exclaimed, "Lock me up, I just killed Pat Garrett."[37]

Sure enough, about five miles east of Las Cruces the awe-struck deputy discovered the lifeless body of Pat Garrett lying alongside the road, dead from a .45 caliber slug fired into the back of his head. Another .45 bullet had been fired into the upper part of Garrett's stomach. Adamson, who had delivered Brazel to the deputy's office told this story: he had been driving the buggy, Brazel was riding his horse alongside. Garrett and Brazel had been arguing about getting Brazel's goats off of Garrett's ranch when Adamson stopped the buggy to urinate. Garrett also stepped out of the buggy. Adamson said he was standing in front of the buggy urinating while Garrett was standing behind doing the same thing. He said it was at that point that he heard a pistol shot, turned around, and witnessed Brazel firing the second shot. Then he relieved Brazel of his .45 pistol and delivered him to Deputy Lucero.

New Mexico Attorney General James M. Hervey was suspicious of Adamson's tale. Plus the young, simple-minded Wayne Brazel just didn't seem like the fearless kind of gunslinger who would challenge Pat Garrett. But, on the other hand, Adamson and his outlaw, in-law kin, Jim Miller, did. Dr. J. J. Bush of El Paso, a friend of Garrett's, wrote New Mexico Governor George Curry with a chilling assessment of Miller, whom he claimed to have known intimately for years. Dr. Bush said:

> He is today the most dangerous man in the whole Southwest. He is deep and burrows beneath the surface like a mole. He is either an open face-to-face gun fighter or a midnight assassin as the case may be. He is a chief of conspirators and a planner of dark deeds.[38]

On the day of Garrett's funeral Attorney General Hervey and Captain Fred Fornoff, chief of the New Mexico Mounted Police, had Adamson take them back to the kill site, which was located at the bottom of the Alameda Arroyo. A steep bank rose up from the north side of the road. Along the south side of the road there was a clump of thick brush, and that's where Hervey found a new shell casing lying on the ground. But according to Adamson's account of the shooting, Brazel had fired the fatal shots while standing in the road just behind Garrett—the first bullet hitting Garnett in the back of his head. When they returned, Hervey remarked to Fornoff that Adamson's story just didn't sound right. He wanted to have the matter thoroughly investigated. But, unfortunately, supposedly on account of a lack of funds, such an investigation was never conducted.

Wayne Brazel was put on trial the first week of May 1909. It was a one-day trial, and it was a farce. Inexplicably, the prosecution did not even call to the witness stand the sole eyewitness, Carl Adamson. Fifteen minutes after the jury retired, it returned with a "not guilty" verdict.

No one else was ever tried, or even indicted, for Pat Garrett's murder. The question remains: was Wayne Brazel really the man who killed Pat Garrett, or was he just the pawn who was manipulated to hide the guilt of the real killer? Was Deacon Jim Miller that guilty party? Beyond serious dispute, Miller had been summoned to New Mexico to slay the famous lawman. He did receive $1500 for the task. He did conspire with his outlaw in-law Carl Adamson to set up the ambush via the phony cattle pasturage deal, and Adamson was present when Garrett was killed. The case against Jim Miller seems compelling, at least on the surface, and some western historians have so concluded. Other historians, however, have contended that although Miller was hired to do the job, another gunman "jumped the gun" and assassinated Garrett. In addition to Wayne Brazel, other suspects were Print Rhodes, Bill Cox, and Oliver Lee—all prominent area ranchers and bitter enemies of Pat Garrett.

The day after the jury acquitted Wayne Brazel, Bill Cox held a big barbecue celebration out at his ranch. It was attended by cowboys, friends, and ranchers from all over the New Mexico range. Western historians are still debating the issue: who killed Pat Garrett?[39] Whoever it was took the secret to his grave. In any event, as soon as the gunsmoke cleared, Jim Miller rode back to Fort Worth with his saddlebags stuffed with $1500 in cash.

THE ASSASSINATION OF THE EX-DEPUTY US MARSHAL GUS BOBBITT

Back in Fort Worth, Miller received an even more lucrative offer, $2,000, to assassinate a prominent cattleman near Ada, Oklahoma. His name was Angus A. "Gus" Bobbitt. In 1907, before Oklahoma became a state, Bobbitt was a Deputy US Marshal in the Indian Territory near Ada, and had become involved in a feud with Jesse West and Joe Allen, sometime cattlemen, sometime saloon keepers. Their saloon, located nearby, had become notorious as a hangout for outlaws. One Oklahoma historian described it as being "the worst den of iniquity" in the territory "where men of evil name, fame, and reputation congregated for the purposes of cursing, drinking, shooting, and performing unlawful acts," including numerous assaults, illegal sales of liquor to Indians, and eight murders during the last nine months.[40] As time passed the feud simmered and festered. In early 1909, Jesse West and Joe Allen hired Jim Miller to settle the feud once and for all by killing Gus Bobbitt. They paid Miller the $2,000 through their intermediary, Fort Worth livestock trader Berry Burrell, Miller's close friend. Burell, it will be recalled, had testified as a defense witness for Jim Miller during the 1906 Frank Fore murder trial.

February 27, 1909—just two days shy of the first anniversary of the assassination of Pat Garrett on the road to Las Cruces, New Mexico—an assassin patiently waited for Gus Bobbitt on a wagon road seven miles southwest of Ada, Oklahoma. Bobbitt had been to Ada that day and had loaded his wagon with cattle feed. Now, near sundown, he approached his ranch headquarters. The sun had just gone down. Shadows deepened in the hush of evening. In the brush in a dusky hollow alongside the wagon road, Deacon Jim Miller thrust the barrel of his 12 gauge shotgun through the fork of a large elm tree. It was loaded with "00" buckshot. Finally, Bobbitt drew abreast of the brushy hollow. The evening silence was broken. Deacon Jim's double barrel shotgun roared. Twice.

He had just earned his $2,000 fee.

Although mortally wounded, Bobbitt survived long enough to tell his wife that he did not recognize his assassin, but that the man wore unusual attire for a badman of the Old West: "...a striped tie and white collar, and a white handkerchief around his neck." He assumed it was a hired gun, hired by his longtime enemies West and Allen to settle an old score.

Word quickly spread. Infuriated by the craven bushwhacking of their neighbor—a family man, unarmed and up to nothing more sinister than bringing home a load of cattle feed—a frenzied posse formed and picked up the trail of the assassin. The horseback trail wasn't that hard to follow. The bloodthirsty posse followed the trail for thirty miles to the home of a young man named John Williamson. At first, Williamson denied everything, said his horse, a mare, had never left the farm. But the grim-faced pursuers weren't buying it. The horse's hooves matched the tracks they had followed. Finally, after some arm-twisting, a punch or two in the nose, and worse, he confessed that a man paid him $20 for the use of his mare.

"What man?"

"I can't tell—he'd kill me."

"If you don't tell us, we will. What man?"[41]

That's when Williamson went limp, started babbling, and identified the killer: his uncle, Jim Miller.

Deacon Jim Miller, Joe Allen, Jesse West, and Berry Burrell were eventually arrested and lodged in the jail at Ada. Although Miller was captured, indicted, and lodged in the Ada jail, and the prosecution's case looked like a lay-down hand, still Miller, unlike his cellmate accomplices, appeared confident. Even serene. This wasn't his first courthouse rodeo —he had a satchel full of tricks. He'd repeatedly beaten the rap, even when caught red-handed after he'd killed Deputy Marshal Ben Collins.

Bolstering his self-confidence still more was the employment of ace Oklahoma Territory criminal defense lawyer, Moman Pruiett. During Pruiett's long and astonishingly triumphant career, he had defended 342 clients accused of murder, 304 of whom had strolled out of the courtroom free citizens. Only thirty-eight had been found guilty, but none of those swung from the gallows.[42] Miller, of course, was also reassured by the fact that he could depend on his obedient, though raucous, herd of defense witnesses to outnumber and out-swear any team of prosecution witnesses.

Meanwhile, Deacon Jim lounged around the Ada jail, dressed in his formal, black-suited attire, shaved twice a day, had fresh linens sent up for his bed each morning, ordered porterhouse steaks, and tipped the jailer five dollars a day.

Jim Miller may have been serene and self-confident, but his cellmates were not nearly as laid-back or as cocksure of their sunny future. They were, perhaps, more aware of how much the cowardly, back-shooting assassination of their unarmed neighbor had enraged the community. And when those folks learned that Miller and friends had hired the unbeatable Moman Pruiett ...well, that was the last straw—the straw that broke the camel's back. This time the Ada folks were determined to see that Miller would not again walk out of their jail a free man, would not again make a mockery of justice. If the nascent courtroom justice of that day was too feeble to get the job done, then they would. Effective frontier justice would be administered.

The case against the four prisoners was resolved much quicker than Miller and his accomplices had anticipated. And it was not resolved in a courtroom. It would be administered in a livery stable located just behind the jailhouse. Shortly after 2:00 a.m. on Sunday, April 19, 1909, a mob of forty or more masked men arrived at the jail, forced open the jail doors, beat two guards over the head with pistol barrels, bound their hands and feet with baling wire, and then escorted the prisoners to the livery stable where four ropes with nooses were already dangling from the rafters.

Defiant and undaunted to the end, Deacon Jim Miller faced the inevitable. He removed his diamond ring and asked that it be sent to his wife back in Fort Worth. Then he removed his diamond stick pin and requested that it be given to his accommodating jailer. Then he bragged, "Let the record show I've killed fifty-one men."[43]

A noose was then fitted around the neck of each of the four men.

"Let 'er rip," were Deacon Jim Miller's last words.[44]

By the time their mission was finally concluded that April night, a light drizzle of cold rain had set in. The mob quietly dispersed and vanished into the darkness. None of the participants was ever indicted. Not that anybody cared. The gavel of frontier justice had descended on the life and crimes of Deacon Jim Miller.

This time there would be no appeal.[45]

James Brown Miller never lived to watch the sun rise on his forty-eighth birthday.

Figure 25. Jim Miller Hanging

(Public domain. Courtesy of Ada [Oklahoma] *Weekly Democrat,* April 23, 1909.)

Jim Miller had escaped the noose in several murder trials by calling his cast of standby defense witnesses ready to testify on demand and as directed. But after fatally ambushing former Deputy U.S. Marshal Angus A. "Gus" Bobbitt near Ada, Oklahoma, in 1909, an enraged group of locals decided Deacon Jim had dodged the noose one time too many. Jim Miller is the culprit shown here hanging on the left.

On April 20, 1909, after reporting the lynching of Jim Miller and his three cohorts the previous day, the *Ada* [Oklahoma] *Evening News* editor added this comment to his story:

> Lynchings are to be deplored, but Oklahoma juries are permitting too many murderers to escape the penalty of their crimes, while procedure in the courts, with the importance given to trifling technicalities, is making it easy for criminals to escape punishment... In Jim Miller the citizens of Ada...*knew* they had not hanged an innocent man. This fellow from Fort Worth had been a murderer for a quarter of a century yet had always managed to escape justice in the courts of Texas and Oklahoma. He had friends, even among good citizens, and seemed reasonable and unassuming. But behind the attractive mask was a hired killer who murdered in cold blood with unspeakable brutality. He was the personification of a psychopath. Only the vigilantes at Ada were able to stop him.

Was Deacon Jim Miller the killer who assassinated Jim Jarrott? Was he that impeccably attired gentleman who had observed Jim and wife Mollie stroll down the main street of Lubbock a few days before Jim Jarrott was ambushed?

More than three decades would pass before Mollie, then the wife of Monroe Abernathy, received some credible information that Jim Miller was indeed the hired gun who had assassinated her husband on that fateful day in August 1902.

It was 1933 when Monroe Abernathy's cousin, John A. "Catch 'em-Alive, Jack" Abernathy, told the tale of J. W. Jarrott's assassination. Back in 1906, when Jack was the U. S. marshal of the Oklahoma Territory, he, together with U. S. Deputy Marshal Frank Canton and some local lawmen, had arrested Jim Miller near Hobart for the murder of U. S. Deputy Marshal Ben Collins. Marshal Abernathy had then transported his prisoner to jail in Guthrie. Miller became impressed with his captor because Abernathy didn't bother to handcuff him or clamp on leg irons during the railroad journey. As a result, Deacon Jim, who was naturally garrulous and boastful, relaxed and became talkative. It was during that long conversation that Deacon Jim opened up and began to tell stories about some other murders for which he had never been arrested

—including the 1902 assassination of a man named J. W. Jarrott on the South Plains southwest of Lubbock.

When this 1906 conversation occurred, Marshal Abernathy was not familiar with Jim Jarrott or his wife Mollie, nor was he aware that three years after Jarrott's murder, his widow, Mollie, had married his cousin, Monroe Abernathy. Moreover, Jack Abernathy apparently had never been to Lubbock until 1933.

It was during that visit that he had a conversation with John Jarrott, the young man who was the son of Jim and Mollie Jarrott. And it was also then that Jack Abernathy first learned John's father was the Jim Jarrott who Deacon Jim had (in 1906) confessed to assassinating back in August 1902. He also learned that John Jarrott's mother, Mollie, had married his cousin, Monroe Abernathy, after Jim Jarrott's death. When John Jarrott related this story to his step-father and his mother, Jack Abernathy went on to disclose to them all the details of Miller's confession.

Since Deacon Jim Miller had long since met his end at the end of a rope in Ada, Oklahoma, ex-marshal Jack Abernathy was no longer legally nor morally bound by his pledge of confidentiality to keep secret anything Miller had disclosed to him. Miller's detailed account of the Jarrott assassination had been triggered by Jack Abernathy's question: "Do you remember the hardest man to kill in your experience?"

His reply: "Jim Jarrott," adding he had to shoot the unarmed victim five times.

Jack Abernathy then recounted the details of the Jarrott murder as told to him by Miller. He named his assigned victim: Jim Jarrott. He accurately gave the location: on the South Plains several miles southwest of Lubbock. He described the kill site: a "pasture tank" between the twin tower mills. He had tied and hidden his horse behind the mound of dirt excavated to form the pasture tank and patiently awaited the victim. When Jarrott came driving up to the tank to water his horses Miller rose from his hiding place behind the mound and shot him, but didn't kill him. Jarrott fell or jumped off the wagon and started running toward the tank. Miller followed, shooting Jarrott three more times before the final kill-shot, and then left Jarrott's body lying in the tank. At that point, Miller added a comment of questionable sincerity: "I hated to do this when I saw that Jarrott was not armed."[46]

Miller then continued to give Abernathy the whole story of the Jarrott assassination. His account tallied with the crime scene as observed by lawmen and others when Jarrott's body was discovered: the cartridge hulls ejected from Miller's rifle and strewn along the path taken by Miller in pursuit of the fleeing Jarrott, the blood spots on the ground and Jarrott's tracks leading from the wagon to the pond where his body was found, and a horse's stomp marks on the ground where Miller said he had tied his horse while waiting for Jarrott—the stomp marks evidencing the fact that the horse had stomped to shoo off flies that were obviously annoying him during the prolonged wait in the hot summer.

Other evidence exists that tends to corroborate the authenticity of Jim Miller's confession. As we shall soon discover in the next chapter, official Terry County records prove that Miller was in the vicinity of Jarrott's assassination near the time of the murder—both shortly before and shortly afterwards. Also, in his confession Miller claimed he had been paid $500 (his standard assassination fee back in 1902) by one rancher for terminating that troublesome sodbuster—paid by a cattleman who was determined not only to get rid of Jarrott but also to teach the rest of those settlers "a hard lesson."[47] He declined, however, to name his employer. (After all, that would have been bad for future business: who would have wanted to hire a loose-lipped assassin?)

But who? Who was the deep-pockets who handed $500 cash to Deacon Jim for his bloody deed? Five hundred dollars in today's money amounts to about $13,254.72. Obviously, the deep-pockets source was somebody a lot richer than some South Plains cowboy who drew a $30 a month paycheck.

Chapter 9

The Man Who Hired the Assassin

"He counted little on law enforcement, believing himself fully capable of handling his own problems."[1]

It was on the afternoon of August 27, 1902, that Deacon Jim Miller assassinated Jim Jarrott at the Twin Mills site approximately twenty-five miles southwest of Lubbock.

Early that morning Grace Cowan, the sixteen-year-old daughter of Lee Cowan (one of Jarrott's Strip settlers), was playing outside the family homestead near the present-day village of Ropesville when she was startled to see a horseman race by headed north. Later that same day—but after the assassination—Grace Cowan once again spied the same horseman race by, but this time headed south away from the Twin Mills.

Although Grace Cowan wasn't able to identify the rider, the sight of a lone horseman racing by out there on the lonely Llano Estacado back in 1902, was an unusual sight indeed, and one sufficient to attract the attention of anyone. Especially if the horseman was racing by heading one direction in the morning and then later the same day, racing by heading the opposite direction. Although she wasn't able to positively identify the rider, she later testified she was certain that it was the same horse and the same rider and that they were headed north on the morning toward the Twin Mills and south the same afternoon headed away from the Twin Mills. But who was that man? What was he up to? And why was he in such a hurry? Where was he going?[2]

Almost thirty years later it became clear that the horseman Grace Cowan witnessed racing by her home that afternoon was Deacon Jim Miller, that he had just assassinated Jim Jarrott, and that he was in a hurry to flee the scene of his crime to prevent being identified and implicated. But what was his destination that afternoon?

By weaving together all the strands of circumstantial evidence that came to light during the thirty years after Jim Jarrott was assassinated, Deacon Jim Miller's destination that fateful afternoon as he fled the scene of his crime would become apparent. And, in turn, that would provide a valuable clue in identifying the man who paid Deacon Jim Miller his $500 blood money fee.

Meantime, while that history-mystery was simmering in the pot, another Llano Estacado history-mystery involving Jim Miller was beginning to unreel. Irrefutable evidence not only from eyewitnesses but also from the official Terry County Deed Records proves that Deacon Jim Miller was present in the immediate South Plains area at the time of the August 1902 assassination and on into the late winter of 1902 and early spring of 1903. It was during those latter months that the Deacon had taken advantage of a golden opportunity to change his costume, take center stage, and display his finely honed skills as an actor in a con artist drama—a complicated rangeland swindle that we will hereinafter refer to as the bizarre "deed-shuffle scam." The targeted victim of that scam? It wasn't a sodbuster this time; it was a South Plains cattleman. But which cattleman? And who was Jim Miller's employer? The same money-bags who paid him $500 to dispose of J. W. Jarrott? Or somebody else? Time would tell. And a connection would be revealed. An important one.

NARROWING THE SUSPECT LIST

Back to the first question: who did hire Deacon Jim Miller to assassinate Jim Jarrott? In 1903 a Lubbock County grand jury indicted four Lake-Tomb cowboys: William Barrington for murder, alleging that he was the triggerman, along with Ben Glaser, Morgan Bellow, and B. F. Nix indicted as accomplices.[3] The indictments were later dismissed as being without merit or evidentiary support. Upon further reflection, it also became clear that the assassination carried the earmarks of a professional killer, not the imprint of a range cowboy. Jim Miller, during his 1906 "confidential" conversation with Oklahoma Territory US marshal John "Catch'em-Alive" Jack Abernathy, bragged that he had been paid $500 for his services.[4] No South Plains ranch hand drawing $30 per month cowboy wages could possibly have come up with that much cash.

Next to consider: did Jim Jarrott have any known enemies? None. Except the cattle kings on the South Plains who viewed Jarrott and his settlers as intruders on "their" territory—"their" territory by right of first possession. They viewed those intruders with disdain yes, but also viewed them as a long-term threat to their bank accounts if those four-section invaders kept on coming.

Considering that question narrows the suspect list considerably. In 1900, there were only a few large ranches on the South Plains, and prior to Jarrott's murder only two of those owners had filed formal complaints against Jarrott, his homesteaders, and Jarrott's friend, Charles Rogan, commissioner of the State of Texas General Land Office. Those complaints were filed by David DeVitt, owner of the Mallet Ranch, and by the attorney for the non-resident owners of the Lake-Tomb Cattle Company. Yet both owners of those ranches appeared to have been satisfied to limit their challenges against Jarrott and his settlers to filing protests with the land commissioner and filing civil suits alleging that Jarrott's settlers were really only land rush profiteers—not genuine Four-Sections Act homesteaders.

However, there were other cattle barons who had yet to weigh in on the ranchers vs. the homesteaders battle. In 1900, there were only three big ranch owners in Terry County who called the South Plains home and who actually lived at the headquarters of their ranches. One of whom was M. V. "Pap" Brownfield.[5]

Another factor to be taken into account: undoubtedly by the time those four Lake- Tomb cowboys were indicted in 1903, everybody in the closely knit South Plains ranching community, as well as their associates, had become aware of the identity of the man who hired Jarrott's killer—and that included those four falsely accused Lake-Tomb cowboys imprisoned in the Lubbock County jail. That being the case, which cattle baron would have had the greatest incentive to make sure that the accused triggerman, William Barrington, kept his mouth shut? Next inquiry: who was the man who secured the release of William Barrington by executing his $5,000 bail bond? Logic leads to the unavoidable conclusion that William Barrington's bondsman wanted to be absolutely certain that Barrington kept his mouth shut. Barrington's bail bondsman turned out to be Marion Virgil "Pap" Brownfield.

Marion Virgil "Pap" Brownfield was born in Iowa on January 25, 1854, son of Joseph Collins and Martha Chipps Brownfield, as one of nine children born to that pioneer family.[6] They later moved to Missouri and then migrated to Dallas County, Texas, in the early 1860s. On November 1, 1862, Pap's father, Joe Brownfield, enlisted in the Confederate army. He served in Company "D," Sixth Texas Cavalry, until he was captured by Union forces at La Fourche, Louisiana, on June 23, 1863, but was later paroled upon taking an oath not to return to military duty—an oath that he didn't keep. He promptly rejoined the Confederate army and served the rest of the war.[7]

Shortly after the end of the Civil War, fourteen-year-old M. V. "Pap" Brownfield ran away from home and ended up in Dallas where he found employment as a wagon driver hauling freight from Sedalia, Missouri, to Dallas. He soon quit that job and became a cowboy, driving herds of cattle from Texas to railheads in Dodge City and Abilene, Kansas. According to the Brownfield family tales that "Pap" passed down to his descendants—tales in which he obviously embellished the truth in order to improve the story while burnishing his role in the yarn—young Brownfield associated with "wild characters" during those chaotic and lawless years following the Civil War. He, crossed trails with the likes of Frank and Jesse James, the Daltons, and others who became notorious outlaws including Sam Bass and John Wesley Hardin. He claimed that while the James brothers were never with him on the same cattle drives, they had—at least to hear Pap tell the tale—been with herds just ahead or just behind him. He later regaled his family with tales of saloon shootouts in Abilene, Kansas, during one of which he narrowly escaped a fusillade of flying lead when some wild, booze-soaked cowboy on a binge shot out the lights and kept on pulling the trigger. Pap dived behind a beer barrel. When the smoke cleared, two other saloon patrons lay dead on the floor, and there were bullet holes in Pap's beer barrel shield.[8]

During those years, Pap claimed he was friends with the outlaw Sam Bass. Both shared a passion for horse racing, and together they made the rounds of a number of area horse races. According to a tale Pap later spun to his granddaughter, Sam Bass really wasn't that "hard faced desperado" he'd been made out to be "in song and story." According to Brownfield:

> [Sam Bass] was simply a reckless, hard-riding young cowboy, who loved horse racing and dancing, and dangerous only when he had one drink too many.[9]

Figure 26. Sam Bass

(Courtesy of Robert G. McCubbin Jr.)
Notorious Texas outlaw. Sam Bass and Pap Brownfield enjoyed going to horse races together. According to Pap, Sam Bass wasn't the "hard-faced desperado" he had been made out to be "in song and story." Instead he was just "a reckless hard-riding young cowboy, dangerous only when he'd had a drink too much."

If that was really the case, then Sam Bass must have had a lot more than one drink too many when he and his gang pulled off all those robberies of stagecoaches and trains, including a whopping $60,000 loot in newly minted gold coins they extracted from a Union Pacific train on September 21, 1877, near Omaha, Nebraska.[10] The next year Sam Bass decided to add bank robbery to his resume. That proved to be a disastrous decision. On July 21, 1878, the gang attempted to rob a bank in Round Rock, Texas. In a shootout with lawmen one deputy sheriff was killed, another lawman was seriously wounded and Bass was fatally wounded.[11]

On January 6, 1876, Pap married Ann Elizabeth Hornbeck in Fort Worth. She was the daughter of Robert and Angeline Anderson Hornbeck. Pap Brownfield's family legend continued: Pap's mother-in-law, Angeline Anderson Hornbeck, was related to the notorious killer, Bloody Bill Anderson, who, together with his father-in-law, Robert Hornbeck, rode with the infamous William Clark Quantrill during his hit-and-run raids in Kansas free soil territory—raids that resulted in the slaughter of men, women, and children. Captain Quantrill reached the peak of his infamy when, in August 1863, he led nearly 500 of his raiders in an attack of Lawrence, Kansas, then burned and looted the town and left 200 civilians dead in its wake. Bloody Bill Anderson was the most vicious of Quantrill's guerilla leaders. Later, during the Civil War, Robert Hornbeck soldiered with the Tenth Missouri Cavalry.[12]

When Pap Brownfield married Elizabeth Hornbeck in 1876, he bought a ranch near Fort Worth in Tarrant County, Texas. Then, eight years later, in 1884, Pap sold that ranch and he and his brothers Joe and Willie moved farther west and bought the sprawling Turkey Track ranch west of Abilene, Texas, along Fish Creek in Nolan County.

At that point Pap began breeding and training racehorses. He partnered with Nolan County Sheriff Jim Newman, who was also a racehorse enthusiast. Meanwhile Pap's oldest son, A. M. "Dick" Brownfield, and Dick's younger brother, Almer Brownfield, took an active part in training and riding the racehorses.[13]

For several years, all went well. In the early 1890s however, Pap Brownfield and his good friend and racehorse partner, Sheriff Jim Newman, had a disagreement over the breeding of their racehorses. That disagreement soon spiraled into a full-fledged feud. It got even worse when the next sheriff's election rolled around. Never one to turn the other cheek, Pap Brownfield actively campaigned for Newman's opponent. Despite Brownfield's support, his candidate was defeated. That's when Sheriff Newman and Brownfield began exchanging threats and "carrying guns for each other."

Fortunately, neighboring Sheriff Charley Tom from Stanton in nearby Martin County, a noted peacemaker who had defused more than one volatile frontier showdown, stepped in and prevented a killing. He negotiated a temporary truce between the men and persuaded them to agree on a peace plan: the two feudists would draw cards and the man drawing the low card would be obliged to sell his property in Nolan County and leave the area. That not only avoided a deadly gun battle but also provided an acceptable path of retreat for the loser, one that would permit him to liquidate his assets and leave the Nolan County area without tarnishing his reputation or publicly disgracing himself—matters of utmost importance to frontiersmen of that time and place.

RELOCATING ON THE SOUTH PLAINS

At the drawing, Pap drew the low card, and honored his agreement by selling off his horses, cattle, land, and other holdings and departing.[14] In 1896, he resurfaced on the South Plains and resumed his ranching career in Lynn and Terry County including fifty-two sections of unfenced rangeland, which he leased from the State of Texas in the southeast part of Terry County, locating his headquarters on the "Lost Draw." At that time, Texas charged cattle magnates on the South Plains three cents per acre for five or ten year leases with the leaseholder having an option to renew the lease unless a settler expressed a desire to buy a homestead.

A part of Pap's fifty-two-section ranch extended westward to the center of Terry County where the county seat of Brownfield would later be located. That part of his range lay adjacent to, and just to the south of, state lands leased to a fellow rancher, D. J. Howard. Pap Brownfield and D. J. Howard became friends and business partners, running cattle on their adjacent pastures. The friendship and business partnership between Pap Brownfield and D. J. Howard didn't last long. It was doomed to be a replay of Pap's friendship/partnership with Nolan County Sheriff Jim Newman, which, as noted, had soured and almost turned deadly. By 1902, Brownfield and Howard had become bitter enemies, Brownfield accusing Howard of overstocking and overgrazing the pasture. Since no fences divided their leased pastures, overgrazing by Howard inevitably resulted in overgrazing both Howard's and Brownfield's ranges. Their partnership was terminated in acrimony.[15]

Both Pap Brownfield and D. J. Howard were hardheaded, determined, fearless, and hot-tempered men. A feud ignited and was nearing the boiling point when a third party arrived on the scene. In March 1902, Pap Brownfield's twenty-five-year-old son, A. M. "Dick" Brownfield, accompanied by his young bride, Seleta Jane Daugherty, age twenty-one, and their baby daughter, Lois, arrived on the scene in a covered wagon. Seleta Jane was the daughter of Frank Daugherty, an itinerant blacksmith. Pap had attempted to persuade his son to marry the daughter of a prominent Fort Worth banker, but all in vain. For Dick, love trumped money. He married Seleta.[16] Dick promptly constructed a two-room prairie home for his family, freighting lumber by wagon from the nearest railhead, that being the Big Spring village ninety miles south of their cabin. In the summer of 1902, Dick built his home on the edge of his father's "school land" lease and near the boundary of Howard's land.

Figure 27. Map "Where It All Happened"

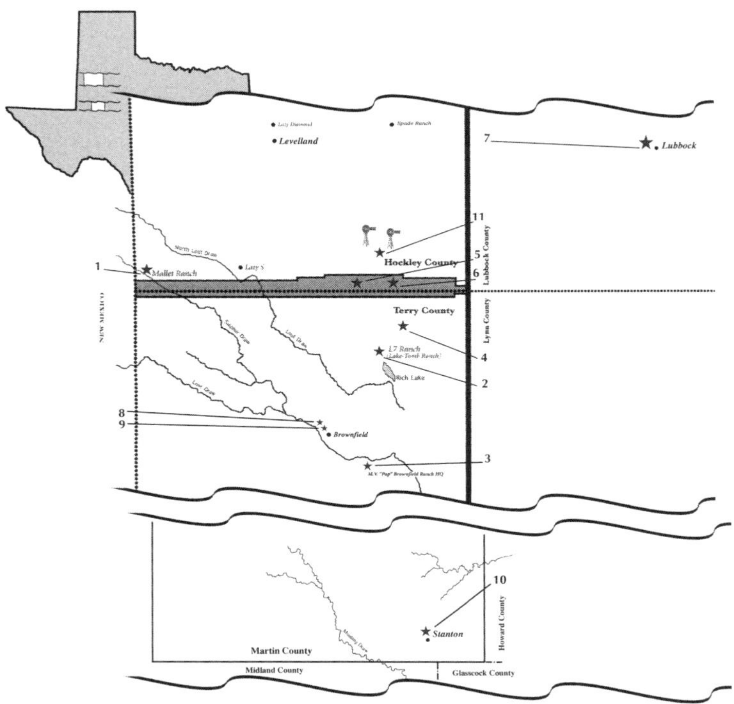

(Map drawn by John Hope. Author's collection.)

Key locations on map identified by numbers.

1. Headquarters of cattle baron David DeVitt's Mallett Ranch. April 1902.

2. Headquarters of Chicago-based Lake-Tomb Cattle Company's sprawling L7 Ranch. April 1902.

3. First headquarters of cattle baron M. V. "Pap" Brownfield's large cattle operations. April 1902.

4. Location of Ward Jarrott's "community house" dugout and grounds where his brother J. W. Jarrott's first group of homesteaders "lit and hitched" while awaiting the Texas General Land Office to set a date when they could file their four-section claims on "the Strip" on the South Plains of Llano Estacado. January 1902.

5. Location of the four-section homestead claim of Jim W. Jarrott and wife Mollie, filed on the Hockley County portion of "the Strip." April 24, 1902.

6. Location of the four-section homestead claim of A. W. Blankenship and wife Mary, filed on the Hockley County portion of "the Strip." April 24, 1902.

7. The Lubbock County clerk's office. That's where the first eight of J. W. Jarrott's homestead clients (including himself and A. W. Blankenship) filed their four-section claims on the Strip land located in Hockley County on April 24, 1902.

8. Location of those four **school** sections of land in Terry County over which Dick Brownfield and D. J. Howard engaged in a three-month sit-in battle to occupy the "first chair" position when the county clerk opened his door at 8:00 a.m. on the morning of February 7, 1903, and accepted the bid of the "first chair" occupant. November 1902 to February 7, 1903.

9. Location of those four **railroad** sections in Terry County, which were the subject of consummate conman Deacon Jim Miller's classic

swindle known as "the deed shuffle scam" by which on January 23, 1903, he extracted legal title to those four sections from its owner, D. J. Howard (who received not a penny), and then lateraled the title off to Fort Worth banker, W. H. Fisher, who then on March 7, 1903, lateraled the title off to D. J. Howard's despised enemy, Dick Brownfield. January 23, 1903-March 7, 1903.

10. The district court of Martin County located in the town of Stanton. That's when and where D. J. Howard filed his law suit against his hated enemy, Dick Brownfield, after it dawned on him that he had been swindled out of his four railroad sections by Deacon Jim Miller's "deed shuffle scam"—title to which ended up in Dick Brownfield's hands. At the trial, a fellow who Dick Brownfield later claimed he had never seen before showed up "out of the blue" and gave suit-winning testimony on behalf of Dick Brownfield. His name was Jim Miller—Deacon Jim Miller. June 1903.

11. Location of the "Twin [Wind] Mills" on the L7 Ranch. That's where "nester" leader J. W. Jarrott was assassinated on August 27, 1902. **Note:** The assassination site is located directly north of M. V. "Pap" Brownfield's ranch headquarters.

Meanwhile, a part of the state lands that the State of Texas had leased to Howard consisted of "railroad sections," and the state had recently deeded four of those sections to a railroad. The railroad promptly sold the four sections to an individual named Z. T. Joiner. On January 17, 1902, Joiner sold those four sections to Howard.[17] About that time, the state gave notice to Pap Brownfield that when his state lease expired on four interlocking "school sections" in February 1903, the Texas General Land Office (GLO) would put them up for sale under the Four-Sections Act. Those eight sections—the four railroad sections Howard had just purchased and the four school sections that Pap Brownfield had leased but were coming up for sale in February 1903—composed an interlocking eight-section block of land that both Howard and Brownfield were determined to own—determined to own "come hell or high water," as frontiersmen of that day used to say.

D. J. Howard wasted no time in warning Pap Brownfield to stay out of the way, that he intended to buy those four school sections. Pap, however, had other ideas. He not only intended to buy those four school sections, he also began plotting an ingenious scheme to swindle Howard out of his four interlocking railroad sections—the ones that Howard had just purchased from Joiner.

WINDMILL THAT WALTZED ACROSS THE PRAIRIE

The first move by Pap Brownfield—for reasons that will soon become apparent—was to assign his state lease on his four school sections to son, Dick, and thus allow Dick to assume the role of his front man in the upcoming range war with D. J. Howard. Those eight interlocking sections in the middle of Terry County included the railroad section (now owned by Howard) where the county seat town (Brownfield) would later be located. Dick had built his home on a school section that was adjacent to one of Howard's railroad section. And, by chance, it was on that railroad section that Howard and Brownfield had previously drilled a water well and erected a gigantic forty-foot Eclipse windmill tower. Pap wanted to move the mill and tower a few hundred feet to a site on his school section—the one where Dick's home was located. Howard ordered Pap to leave it alone, and uttered other typical threats—threats that were a waste of Howard's time and breath. Pap was unfazed and undeterred. In response, he and Dick targeted Howard as the butt of a bit of chicanery with comedic overtones. They "bided their time" until Howard and his family left on a trip. Much to Howard's amazement, when he returned home, his windmill—tower, mill, fantail, and all—had mysteriously disappeared. Well, not "disappeared" exactly. But it had somehow, as if by magic, taken wings, and flown a few hundred feet over into Brownfield's territory.

Years later Dick chuckled and related how he and Pap had worked their magic. It went like this: first, they hitched two teams of horses to two wagons that were loaded with two heavy beams and other tools, then they hauled them to the windmill site. They removed the bolts that fastened the windmill tower legs to four embedded corner posts. They jacked up the tower and placed the two heavy beams underneath them. (The beams were to serve as skids.) With that done, they hooked the skids to the two wagons. Then they slowly, very slowly, dragged the whole tower and mill, still standing upright, across the prairie to the Brownfield lease where Pap had just drilled a well bore.

Not satisfied with that, and just for good measure, they returned to the Howard well site (now devoid of a tower and mill) where they unearthed the four remaining corner posts and proceeded to drop them down the well bore—just to make sure that if Howard wanted to establish another water producing windmill he would be obliged to hire somebody to dig another water well bore and then buy another windmill.

Thinking back on the trick years later, Dick laughed and remarked that he hoped "no drunk observed a forty-foot windmill tower creeping across the open prairie in an upright position."[18] Pap Brownfield's extralegal solutions to problems thus bypassed lawmen, lawyers, expenses, and delays while ensuring success. And revenge.

THE GIANT ELM TREE THAT VANISHED

The jaw-dropping spectacle of a giant upright windmill tower doing a slow waltz across the prairie was not the only imaginative extralegal ploy Pap Brownfield concocted to resolve difficulties with neighbors. Once, years later, when Pap was living in the fledgling town of Brownfield (named in his honor), the town fathers met and agreed to construct sidewalks in the downtown area. This necessitated the removal of several trees in front of some homes. One citizen, W. B. Downing, refused to allow the city to remove his favorite tree, a large elm. Pap Brownfield rode to the rescue. Once again he "bided his time" and when the recalcitrant homeowner left town for a few days, Pap was ready. He took his saw, ambled over to the neighbor's front yard, cut that giant elm tree down and dragged it away.[19] The sidewalk project was soon completed. Once again, as Pap viewed matters, there was no need wasting a lot of time and money on lawyers and courts, meantime waiting around hoping that those "lawyer fellers" would come up with the desired resolution.

THE "FIRST CHAIR" BATTLE FOR THE FOUR SCHOOL SECTIONS

In the spring of 1902, the Texas General Land Office (GLO) posted notice that four *school* sections located in Terry County would come up for sale under the Four-Sections Act at 8:00 a.m. on Monday, February 17, 1903—would be sold to the man holding the "first chair" position at the county clerk's door. At the time notice was given, Pap Brownfield held the property under a lease from the state. Pap immediately assigned his state lease to son Dick Brownfield and told him to secure and hold that "first chair" position until the clerk's back door opened for bids. Meanwhile, the Brownfields anticipated trouble with D. J. Howard, and Howard, true to form, warned the Brownfields to "stay away" when those school sections were placed on the market. Pap and Dick, however, true to form, were unfazed and undeterred.

The battle to seize and hold that first chair would prove to be neither quick nor easy. For openers, although the four school sections in question were located in Terry County, the "first chair" battle would not be held in that county since Terry County was an unorganized county at that time and was attached to Martin County for judicial purposes. Therefore the battleground would take place in the village of Stanton, county seat of Martin County, approximately ninety miles southeast of the four school sections. And ninety miles was a considerable distance in those days when transportation was limited to the back of a horse. To get from anywhere in Terry County to the town of Stanton in one day was almost impossible.[20]

In November 1902, Dick Brownfield dispatched two of his cowboys to the clerk's office in Stanton with instructions to seize and hold the backdoor position. As soon as D. J. Howard heard about it, he sent two of his cowboys to Stanton, and the battle began and lasted all of that blizzard-swept winter until the target date of February 17, 1903, during which times skullduggery, threats, tricks, and fistfights broke out that frequently required refereeing services by Martin County Sheriff Charley Tom (the noted "peacemaker" sheriff). A last minute trick by Brownfield's cowboys won the battle. And title to those four school sections.

Once title to those four school sections had been secured, Pap and Dick Brownfield refocused on tricking title from Howard out of his four interlocking *railroad* sections—those four railroad sections that Howard had just purchased from T. J. Joiner. Successful trickery there would require a convoluted bit of chicanery—and a sucker punch that Howard never saw coming.

THE DEED-SHUFFLE SCAM TO GET THE FOUR RAILROAD SECTIONS

February 17, 1903, was the date the Brownfield faction defeated the Howard contingent in the "first chair" battle for the four school sections. Even while Dick Brownfield was engaged in that contest for the four school sections, he had (no doubt with the advice and consent of Pap) already set in motion a clandestine scheme to swindle D. J. Howard out of his four interlocking railroad sections—and do so without having to pay Howard one dime. As previously noted, the secret plot to deprive Howard of his title to the four railroad sections might be more accurately described as the "deed-shuffle" scam. To bait the hook, a master conman was summoned. His name was James B. "Deacon Jim" Miller.

Deacon Jim made his first appearance on the scene as a con artist on January 17, 1902. That's when D. J. Howard bought those four railroad sections from Z. T. Joiner. The deed from Joiner to Howard recited that

Howard had paid Joiner the sum of $896 for the four section block.[21] The Joiner-to-Howard warranty deed also revealed that it was witnessed, signed, and authenticated by a notary public and certified with an imprint of an official State of Texas notary seal. The alleged notary public was an unsworn imposter named "James B. Miller." Once again Jim Miller put to good—though illegal—use his stolen notary public seal. Since Miller rendered his notary public service to Howard at no cost, he thus established his friendship and credibility with Howard.

On August 27, 1902—seven months after Deacon Jim Miller stamped his notary public seal on the Joiner-to-Howard deed—the Deacon completed another assignment in Terry County. This took place about fifteen miles northeast of Howard's four railroad sections. For that assignment Deacon Jim switched hats from that of a conman back to that of a hitman. And that's when he assassinated J. W. Jarrott.

Then, six months later on January 23, 1903, Miller switched back to his conman role and persuaded D. J. Howard to sign a deed conveying to him those four railroad sections. No cash down. Apparently fearing that Howard might reconsider and renege on his agreement to execute a formal typewritten deed conveying those four sections of land to Miller for no cash down, only an assignment of "a certain promissory note for $3,900," Miller persuaded Howard to sign a handwritten agreement to execute such a formal typewritten deed. The handwritten agreement was dated January 14, 1903, eight days before the formal Warranty Deed was actually executed on January 23, 1903. (See copy of the handwritten agreement below.) The only consideration Howard received for the conveyance was a bogus $3,900 promissory note.[22]

Figure 28. Deed Contract between J. B. Miller and D. J. Howard

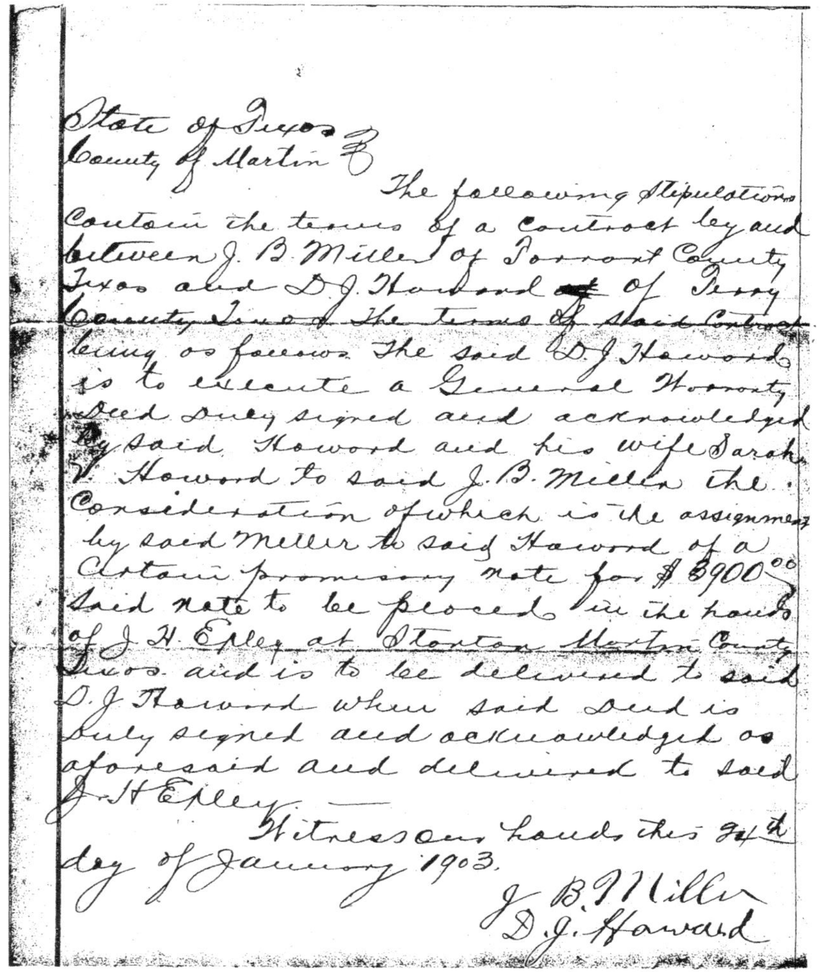

State of Texas }
County of Martin }

The following Stipulations Contain the terms of a contract by and between J. B. Miller of Tarrant County Texas and D. J. Howard of Terry County Texas. The terms of said Contract being as follows. The said D. J. Howard is to execute a General Warranty Deed duly signed and acknowledged by said Howard and his wife Sarah V. Howard to said J. B. Miller the Consideration of which is the assignment by said Miller to said Howard of a Certain promissory note for $3900.00 said note to be placed in the hands of J. H. Epley at Stanton Martin County Texas and is to be delivered to said D. J. Howard when said Deed is duly signed and acknowledged as aforesaid and delivered to said J. H. Epley —

Witness our hands this 24th day of January 1903.

J. B. Miller
D. J. Howard

(Public record in Terry County, Texas, deed records.)

James B. Miller (aka "Deacon Jim Miller") was not only an infamous assassin for hire, but also a polished conman. This handwritten 1903 contract for deed was his first step in swindling D. J. Howard out of four sections of land in Terry County, Texas, where the town of Brownfield is now located.

Miller apparently persuaded Howard it really wasn't necessary for him to guarantee payment of the $3,900 note since it was executed by a prominent, Merkel, Texas, banker named T. J. Coggin and was also secured by a lien on a large tract of land Coggin owned in East Texas. Plus, the note was payable in full within only ninety days from date. End result: Howard swallowed the bait—hook, line, and sinker. Miller was now the sole owner of Howard's four railroad sections, and he hadn't paid Howard anything and wasn't liable to Howard for any amount of money. Plus Miller didn't risk losing title via foreclosure on the Howard's four-sections even if Coggin defaulted on the payment of the $3,900 note. Howard, meanwhile, ended up in the cesspool—victim of Deacon Jim Miller's master flimflam. As it turned out, T. J. Coggin—the fellow who posed as a "Merkel banker" and who had executed that $3,900 note that Deacon Jim had assigned to Howard. Well, lo and behold, he really wasn't a Merkel banker; he was a crook and, as we have already discovered, a bosom buddy cohort of Jim Miller. And that large block of East Texas land Coggin had pledged to secure payment of his $3,900 promissory note? That turned out to be a large worthless chunk of swamp. But that didn't really make any difference either since, contrary to Deacon Jim's verbal assurance to Howard, Coggin didn't have title to that dismal swamp in the first place.

Coggin's bogus ninety-day promissory note came due March 31, 1903. The due date came and went and, of course, Coggin was nowhere to be found. That's when it finally dawned on Howard that he was the victim of a master scam, that he was left holding an empty sack while wiping egg off his face. Howard, who had obviously been so intoxicated by the prospect of grabbing the whopping sum of $3,900 (way yonder above the market value of land he had just bought for $896), that he hadn't even taken the rudimentary precaution of inserting a foreclosure provision in his deed to Miller guaranteeing him the right to foreclose and recover title to his four railroad sections if the $3,900 note wasn't paid in full when due.

However, between the time Howard executed the deed to Miller on January 17, 1903, and when the $3,900 note became due and default was made on March 31, 1903, the bizarre deed-shuffle had already shifted into high gear. On January 30, 1903, Miller sold the four sections to a Fort Worth banker named W. H. Fisher. The deed recited that Miller received $4,100 cash from Fisher. Nothing in the deed obligated Fisher to pay Howard anything in the event Coggin defaulted on his $3,900 note to Howard.[23]

Fisher, in turn, on March 7, 1903—less than a month before Coggin's $3,900 note became due—executed another deed conveying clear title to Howard's four railroad sections to Dick Brownfield for a recited consideration of $800 cash. No lien reserved. And no obligation for Brownfield to pay Howard anything if Coggin defaulted.[24]

It was obvious that much more was going on behind the scenes of this deed-shuffle than was apparent from recitations in the recorded deeds. Why would a prominent Fort Worth banker (Fisher or any other Fort Worth banker) buy four sections of land with a market value of about $896 located way out on the South Plains of Texas more than 300 miles from Fort Worth and pay Jim Miller (or anybody else) $4,100 cash and then about a month later lateral off the same tract of land to another man (Dick Brownfield) for a mere $800 as recited in banker Fisher's deed to Dick Brownfield? The convoluted and irrational recitations made no sense. What it did evidence was that the parties—Jim Miller, T. J. Coggin, W. H. Fisher, and Dick Brownfield—were all playing on the same team. The strong odor of a rotten, decaying rodent was unmistakable. Banker Fisher served Dick Brownfield as a mere conduit—a front man—for the payment of conman Jim Miller's fee for his masterful bit of skullduggery?

And...perhaps Dick Brownfield himself was only a conduit in passing that $4,100 cash fee to Miller. Beyond doubt, the deep-pocket source of that $4,100 cash was Dick Brownfield's father, Pap Brownfield, and he had to have been well acquainted not only with Deacon Jim Miller, but also with the Fort Worth banker W. H. Fisher—and had known them long before the fraudulent deed-shuffle scam was put in play. The fact that both banker Fisher and Jim Miller were residents of Fort Worth at the time is noteworthy, as is the fact that Pap Brownfield had been a resident of Fort Worth, had married a Fort Worth girl, and had owned and operated a ranch near Fort Worth for eight years prior to moving his livestock operations first to Nolan County near Abilene, Texas, and then on to the South Plains. It seems highly unlikely that Pap Brownfield would not have been well acquainted with Fort Worth banker W. H. Fisher in that small, late nineteenth century town. (And, by the way, was W. H. Fisher perchance the man Pap Brownfield referred to when he urged his son, Dick, to marry the daughter of a "Fort Worth banker?") Furthermore, as we have seen in the previous chapter, Deacon Jim Miller had summoned Pap Brownfield as his key defense witness in the sensational 1904 Frank Fore murder trial.

(For a detailed and documented chronicle of events and the timeline see the Appendix.)

D. J. Howard was enraged when he discovered that Dick Brownfield, with a little help from his "chair-sitter" cowboy employees, had tricked him out of his "first chair" seat at the end of the four-month marathon sit-in contest in the distant village of Stanton for the right to buy the four school sections. Now this! Humiliation must have competed with another surge of rage when it finally dawned on Howard that his supposed friend, James Miller, had turned out to be a well-disguised Judas Iscariot who had played him for a sucker and swindled him out of his four railroad sections. Bad as all that was, there was even worse news in store for Howard. His rage must have escalated past ten on the Richter scale when he learned that he had not only been scammed out of title to his four railroad sections but that the title had then been shuffled off to his despised enemies—the Brownfields!

Of course, Howard could have sued Deacon Jim Miller and his cohort T. J. Coggin for perpetrating the fraud and he probably could have won a courtroom battle...if he had had the nerve to challenge Jim Miller, and if he had lived long enough to make it through the front door of the courthouse. But...

"IT DID LOOK A LITTLE FISHY"

That left only Dick Brownfield as a target to sue for monetary damages —and revenge. Even though Dick Brownfield had not guaranteed payment of Coggin's $3,900 note, Howard nevertheless sued him; claimed that Dick was the behind-the-curtains puppeteer of this deed-shuffle fraud, and demanded a judgment. On the face of it, it did appear that Howard had a strong circumstantial evidence case: that the notorious killer and conman Jim Miller was only the front man of the swindle—front man for Dick Brownfield who now held title to, and was the proud owner of Howard's four railroad sections. Not to mention the prior "first-chair" trickery Dick Brownfield, with a little help from his dad, had concocted to deprive him of the four school sections. Howard's fraud lawsuit against Dick Brownfield looked like a winner.

Trial date approached. And that's when, on the eve of trial, a miracle occurred. A miracle of Biblical proportions. At least to hear Dick Brownfield tell the tale. Out of the blue an angel of mercy appeared. An angel perhaps, but a mortal man in appearance: a tall, blue-eyed, well-dressed, well-mannered gentleman who Dick claimed he had never laid eyes on before. The gentleman introduced himself as James B. Miller and explained that he had heard about Howard's unfortunate lawsuit, and apparently motivated by his sincere (albeit recently acquired) dedication to the cause of truth and justice, had volunteered to testify on Dick's behalf. No charge. And so he did: swore that his deal with D. J. Howard was all fair and square, strictly on the up and up, that he himself had been hornswoggled by that rascal Coggin fellow into believing that he really was a reputable Merkel, Texas, banker and that his $3,900 note was genuine and that he really did own that big East Texas swamp.

The witnesses' demeanor was very pleasing and his testimony was very persuasive. The judge dismissed Howard's lawsuit.

Years later, in a 1937 interview by a local Terry County newspaper, Dick recalled the incident, including Miller's "out of the blue" appearance and his dramatic witness-stand performance before the Martin County District Court. Dick reiterated his claim that he had never met Jim Miller until the day he showed up on the steps of the courthouse and volunteered his free services as a defense witness to testify on Dick's behalf. However, toward the end of that interview, Dick finally conceded that his story "... did look a little fishy."[25] Nevertheless it was all true. So Dick insisted.

Figure 29. Alfred Marion "Dick" Brownfield

(Courtesy of the Terry County Historical Commission.)
He arrived in the South Plains in 1902 with his wife and infant daughter in a covered wagon, and settled in Terry County adjacent to his father's ranch. His father was M. V. "Pap" Brownfield.

THEY NAMED THE TOWN "BROWNFIELD"

Timeout for a sidebar of irony. On August 12, 1903, only fifteen days before the first anniversary of the date Deacon Jim Miller had assassinated J. W. Jarrott a few miles to the northeast of the land that was the subject of the deed-shuffle caper and only five months after Dick Brownfield acquired title to those four railroad sections, Dick sold one of those four sections to A. F. Small and W. G. Hardin, frontier town promoters, and they succeeded in promoting the settlement of a village on that site that soon became the county seat of Terry County. Final irony: Small and Hardin named the town "Brownfield" in honor of Pap Brownfield. And so, for a brief spell during the deed-shuffle caper, the master conman Deacon Jim Miller—and also the most notorious, gun-for-hire assassin in the Southwest—had been the sole and lawful owner of all the land upon which the town of Brownfield now occupies.

DEEP POCKETS? OR JUST DECEPTION?

A piece of the deed-shuffle swindle remains for examination. If, as concluded, Dick Brownfield was the puppeteer who pulled the strings, then who was the deep pocket who furnished the $4,100 payoff to Jim Miller? Seems highly unlikely that it was Dick Brownfield, he who had recently arrived on the scene in a covered wagon with his bride and infant daughter. But what about Dick's father Pap Brownfield? The inescapable conclusion is that Pap Brownfield was the deep-pocket source who handed his friend, Deacon Jim Miller, the $4,100 fee for his masterful performance as the con artist who slicked D. J. Howard out of his four railroad sections with his "deed-shuffle" scam. Two reasons: first, the Brownfields ended up owning those four railroad sections and second, swindling D. J. Howard out of his four railroad sections sated Pap Brownfield's craving for revenge against his hated enemy.

But what about the $500 fee somebody paid Deacon Jim Miller to assassinate J. W. Jarrott? Who paid that? Did it come out of the same deep pocket?

In any event, Deacon Jim Miller departed Llano Estacado in 1903 after having successfully completed two financially rewarding missions: the assassination of J. W. Jarrott and the successful "deed-shuffle" swindle of D. J. Howard. He mounted and headed back to his home in Fort Worth, saddlebags packed with cash.

WITNESSES FOR THE DEFENSE

The next year, 1904, proved to be a very busy year for Deacon Jim Miller. It was also during that year that the close ties between Jim Miller and Pap Brownfield were documented. On March 10, 1904, just eighteen months after Miller assassinated J. W. Jarrott, he shot and killed Frank Fore in the toilet room of the Delaware Hotel in Fort Worth. As told in the preceding chapter, after a lengthy trial[26] during which Deacon Jim called to the stand his usual cadre of well-rehearsed on-call witnesses, still his self-defense plea appeared to be weak at best in view of Frank Fore's dying declaration. According to Fore, Miller was the aggressor, and he (Fore) didn't threaten Miller, didn't draw a weapon, and didn't fire a shot. Also, Fore didn't mention anyone else being present in the toilet room when Deacon Jim fired the fatal shots.

No two ways about it, Deacon Jim Miller had to produce an eyewitness to contradict Fore's statement—someone who could testify he also was inside the toilet room at the time, and that Frank Fore really was the aggressor, and that Deacon Jim really was forced to draw and fire his pistol in order to save his life. And not just any ordinary witness. Miller needed a prominent, persuasive, intelligent, credible, and bulletproof eyewitness who could withstand any cross-examination the prosecutor might fire at him.

As we also learned in the preceding chapter, Deacon Jim Miller did come up with such an eyewitness, one he could depend upon to follow the defense script—a prominent cattleman who testified that Fore had precipitated the showdown by attempting to draw his pistol first, that therefore Jim Miller had been forced to draw his weapon and shoot Fore, but did so only in self-defense.

That prominent cattleman—the key eyewitness for Deacon Miller's defense, indeed the *only* eyewitness (unless Deacon Jim Miller later happened to think of another one)—was M. V. "Pap" Brownfield. Or so Deacon Jim Miller contended. In preparation for the upcoming murder trial Miller had a subpoena issued for M. V. Brownfield as a defense witness. In a sworn statement dated May 19, 1904, Miller explained that the reason it was necessary for M. V. Brownfield to appear as his defense witness was that he could not "go safely to trial" without Brownfield's testimony. Under oath Miller then proceeded to outline what he expected to prove by Brownfield's testimony:

> M. V. Brownfield was present in the toilet room in the Delaware hotel in Fort Worth at the time of the difficulty between the defendant and the deceased Frank Fore, in which said Fore was killed and saw all that occurred between them at the time, that Brownfield saw the defendant start to exit the toilet room, that the witness [Brownfield] saw him [Miller] look around in the direction of where Fore was, Fore being within a few feet of him, he paused and Fore walked up and took hold of him [Miller]; that a few words passed between them which witness could not understand; that Fore then jumped back and put his hand behind him and began to draw his pistol, when Fore did that the defendant reached behind him and drew his pistol and brought it to his side and fired without raising the pistol; that Fore then staggered back and fell... that defendant did not fire at deceased after he fell... that defendant made no demonstration to fire his pistol or to shoot at or to injure deceased until the deceased made the motion to draw his pistol as stated above; that when deceased fell he had his pistol out and he fell on it on the floor.[27]

It is worth pausing here to note that Jim Miller executed that sworn statement on May 19, 1904—just three months shy of the second anniversary of the date someone paid Miller $500 to assassinate J. W. Jarrott.

Deacon Jim Miller also subpoenaed many other witnesses during the Fore trial. Prominent among them were two other reliable Miller team members: T. A. "Tom" Morrison, a Colorado City (Mitchell County, Texas) cattleman, and Miller's shady partner, T. J. Coggin, the same T. J. Coggin who just over a year earlier had posed as "Gentleman" Jim Miller's "Merkel banker" friend—the one who assisted Miller in his "deed-shuffle" fraud that swindled D. J. Howard out of his four railroad sections in Terry County—the same four sections that shortly thereafter ended up in the hands of Pap Brownfield's son, Dick Brownfield.

Pap Brownfield did show up for the trial, and he did, in fact, testify that he was an eyewitness to the killing of Frank Fore and that Miller had indeed fired the fatal shot—but only in self-defense. Brownfield went on to explain to the jury that he had just happened to have been in Fort Worth some 300 miles away from his South Plains ranch that day to attend the annual meeting of the Texas Cattle Raisers Association, and that he just happened to have been in the Delaware Hotel lavatory at the time the shooting took place.

During the trial Miller decided that he needed to beef up Pap Brownfield's eyewitness testimony. Consequently that's when he suddenly recalled—contrary to his previous sworn affidavit quotes above —that there really was another eyewitness, a fourth occupant of the toilet room when Miller killed Frank Fore—a Colorado City rancher and faithful Jim Miller team player named T. A. "Tom" Morrison, who, as predicted, appeared and echoed Pap Brownfield's version of events. Morrison also went on to explain that he also just happened to have been in town that day for the cattleman's annual meeting, and also just happened to have been in the Delaware Hotel lavatory at the critical moment.

Figure 30. T. A. Morrison

(Courtesy of Nita Haley Stewart Memorial Library, Midland, Texas. Archives JEH-Y-254)

When Deacon Jim Miller was tried for the 1904 murder of detective Frank Fore in Fort Worth, Miller summoned Morrison and M. V. "Pap" Brownfield as defense witnesses. Both testified that they were eyewitness to the killing. According to Miller's predictions, both testified that Miller had killed Frank Fore—but only in self-defense. Miller was acquitted. Morrison later commented: "When I have trouble with somebody I don't go to no court, but make it a personal matter."

Figure 31. Marion Virgil "Pap" Brownfield

(Courtesy of the Terry County Historical Commission.)
Pioneer Terry County rancher Pap Brownfield didn't believe in wasting time or money on lawyers and judges in order to settle a dispute.

With that additional heft to Miller's punch, the courtroom battle was won. As told in the precious chapter, on May 4, 1906, after a lengthy two-month trial during which Miller paraded his gang of defense witnesses to the stand, including the two prominent cattlemen eyewitnesses—Brownfield and Morrison—the jury took only fifteen minutes to find James B. Miller "not guilty."[28]

THE FAILED PROSECUTION OF J. W. JARROTT'S ASSASSIN

Meanwhile, back in October 1903 in Lubbock, those four Lake-Tomb (L7) cowboys had been indicted for the murder of J. W. Jarrott. They were arrested and jailed. That's when somebody caused a subpoena to be issued for the appearance of Tom Morrison as a defense witness. Who? And why?

Tom Morrison's anticipated appearance as a defense witness in the J. W. Jarrott murder trial appears, at least on the surface, to be somewhat peripheral to the main story. Still, it yields a valuable clue to the identity of the man who hired Jarrott's assassin. Morrison was not only a close ally and an on-call witness for serial killer Deacon Jim Miller, but also a friend of another key Miller witness: M. V. "Pap" Brownfield. The criminal careers of Deacon Jim Miller's associates and "on-call" witnesses including Colorado City rancher Tom Morrison and his sidekick T. J. Coggin continued for a number of years after the 1902 assassination of J. W. Jarrott, the 1904 murder of Frank Fore, and the 1909 lynching death of Jim Miller.[29]

The question: who caused Morrison to be subpoenaed as a witness? And why? Morrison had no known connection with the Jarrott assassination, and there was not a shred of evidence that he was even in the South Plains area at the time. And Morrision's ranch was not located on the South Plains. It was located near Colorado City, more than 120 miles southeast of the Twin Mills site where Jarrott was assassinated. Furthermore, Deacon Jim Miller had not been—and never was—indicted for Jarrott's murder, and was not even a suspect in the Jarrott assassination when he was lynched in 1909. It would be almost thirty years later before Miller became a suspect—that being when Miller's confession to US Marshal Jack Abernathy was made public. Clearly, it wasn't Jim Miller who was responsible for the subpoena for Tom Morrison to appear as a defense witness for the Lake-Tomb cowboys. So why was he subpoenaed? And by whom? Obviously it had have been issued by a man who was confident that his friend, Tom Morrison, could be relied upon to follow the defense script in his testimony if called as a witness when, and if, there was ever a Jarrott murder trial.

All four men indicted for the murder of J. W. Jarrott (including William Barrington, the accused triggerman) were Lake-Tomb cowboys. The cowboys were promptly released after their arrest when bail bonds were posted, but not by the Lake-Tomb ranch owners. Who then posted the bail bonds? And why? And was the man who posted Barrington's bail bond the same man who caused a subpoena to be issued for Tom Morrison's appearance as a defense witness for Barrington? The answer: Yes.

After the grand jury returned indictments falsely accusing the four Lake-Tomb cowboys, the man behind the plot to assassinate J. W. Jarrott —the man who hired Deacon Jim Miller—could ill afford to leave those four innocent cowboys sweating in their jail cells, dangling in doubt in the shadow of the gallows. Wouldn't at least one of those cowboys have been likely to crack and turn state's witness for the prosecution and finger the real villain in order to save his own neck? As previously mentioned, by this time most everyone in the South Plains ranching community must have been aware of the identity of the man who hired the assassin.[30] Could the real mastermind behind the plan afford to take that risk? Wouldn't that man be the one most likely to have posted a bail bond for the indicted triggerman, William Barrington, and then have an experienced defense witness subpoenaed and available to exonerate the accused if it came down to a trial—a real professional "not guilty" witness? Like Tom Morrison? All in an effort to reassure the falsely accused Lake-Tomb cowboy defendants, and thus to guarantee their continued silence. The prominent cattle baron who posted the $5,000 bail bond for the release of William Barrington and who subpoenaed Tom Morrison as a defense witness was M. V. "Pap" Brownfield.[31] Was he the mastermind who hired Deacon Jim Miller to get rid of that trouble-making leader of the nesters, J. W. Jarrott, and with the same bullet deter any prospective sodbusters from invading their cattle kingdom? Teach them that "hard lesson" that none would ever forget.[32] Or so he thought.

A FINAL PIECE OF THE PUZZLE

In retrospect—years later after pieces of the puzzle began fitting together—it turned out that there was an objective eyewitness whose testimony was never questioned. A witness whose testimony not only linked Deacon Jim Miller to the crime, but also pointed to the identity of the man who hired him to do the deed. That witness was Grace Cowan, the sixteen-year-old daughter of one of Jarrott's Strip settlers, Lee Cowan.

As previously noted, the Cowan homestead was located three miles southeast of the Twin Mills near the present village of Ropesville. In the early morning of August 27, 1902, the day Deacon Jim Miller assassinated Jim Jarrott, Grace Cowan witnessed a horseman race past heading north toward the Twin Mills. Late that afternoon, after the murder, she again noticed that same man riding the same horse race past again, but this time heading south.

That man, by his own confession—although posthumously revealed—was Deacon Jim Miller. But where had Miller come from that morning and where was he in such a hurry to get back to that afternoon? What was his destination?

There was only one logical destination located in that direction that was also within riding distance on August 27, 1902. A cattle baron lived there. His ranch headquarters and his home were located on the "Lost Draw" in Terry County twelve miles south of the Cowan family homestead. Obviously, that was where Deacon Jim Miller had come from that morning and where he was headed back to after he had completed his deadly assignment that afternoon. (See "The Setting" map, chapter four).

The cattleman's name: M. V. "Pap" Brownfield.[33]

There was one South Plains cattle baron who had come of age on the Texas frontier during the violent, lawless, and chaotic Reconstruction years following the Civil War. A man who, by his own account, had known and associated with the likes of Frank and Jesse James, Bill Dalton, and other notorious outlaws of the era including Sam Bass and John Wesley Hardin. A man with Fort Worth connections and who was well acquainted with Fort Worth banker W. H. Fisher, and was a friend of and fellow defense witness for Deacon Jim Miller during the Frank Fore murder trial. A man who would not tolerate anybody he viewed as a threat to his honor or his property. A man who hesitated not to use trick or trigger to solve his problems with anyone and do so without wasting time or money on lawyers and judges. A man who hesitated not to cut down a recalcitrant neighbor's tree when the neighbor was out of town or to steal another neighbor's windmill when the man wasn't looking.

> "A man who counted little on law enforcement, believing himself fully capable of solving his own problems."[34]

Perhaps Lubbock lawyer and South Plains historian Chuck Lanehart was on target when in his 2011 *Voice For the Defense* magazine article he posed this question: "Shouldn't the South Plains city of Brownfield be renamed 'Jarrottville'?"[35]

Epilogue

What a Difference an Individual Life Can Make

> History teaches you that it's not all about you. Standing alone on a West Texas prairie reflecting on history makes you realize just how small you are in relation to the generations of people and civilizations who have come before and who will come after you... yet, at the same time, history also teaches you what a difference an individual life can make.
>
> **Lara Fergerson, "Why History Matters: A Story From West Texas."[1]**

Nobody was ever convicted, or even tried, for the cowardly assassination of J. W. Jarrott, and for decades thereafter nobody in the tight-lipped, South Plains frontier community dared speak openly about it. Meanwhile, hostilities between the big ranchers and the settlers continued to seethe just beneath the surface.

The ranchers stubbornly clung to the conviction that regardless of what folks back East thought or what legislators in Austin believed, or whatever fuss those common, sodbustin' peasants kicked up, they, the ranch kings, were entitled to their sprawling empires of grass by right of first possession—a right they had earned. After all, they had double-downed and invested their fortunes in this new land where no previous entrepreneurs had staked out a trail to financial success. They had endured the hardships of the open range—the droughts, the absence of flowing streams, no water wells, the stacked, snow-covered carcasses of their cattle after sub-zero blizzards, the ever-present threat of raging grass fires that swept across the range killing everything in its path, cattle rustlers, the long hard trail drives to distant railheads, the vicissitudes of the cattle market, and the general hardships of day-to-day life on the isolated plains.

Yes, they were there first, and therefore contended that these uninvited, unwanted "soddies" were not only trespassing on their territory, they were encroaching, they were plowing up their grass, they were stringing up those "bob-wire" fences on their free-grass ranges, and they were actually staking out claims of ownership on their turf.[2] More than that even, the cattle barons—and even the cowboys who worked for them—sensed that those nesters "posed a threat to their very way of life."[3]

The ire of the cattlemen's resentment naturally focused on J. W. Jarrott, the leader of these unwanted claim-stakers. Not only had he enlisted an army of invading homesteaders, but he then undertook the task of representing them as their attorney in court battles with the cattlemen. It was no coincidence that Jarrott's assassination on August 27, 1902, happened just on the eve of his upcoming court appearance scheduled for September 16, 1902, when he would defend six of his nester clients who had been sued by the cattlemen faction seeking to nullify the titles to their four-section homesteads.

The rancher who paid Jim Miller to assassinate Jarrott succeeded in his goal of silencing the leader of the nesters—permanently. But he failed completely in achieving his second and larger goal: teaching all those squatters a "hard lesson" and thus scaring them off the cattlemen's domain—scaring them so badly that they would pull up stakes and flee back to wherever they came from.[4] Plus it would, he must have reckoned, deter any future encroachment on ranch turf. In fact, Pap Brownfield's strategy backfired; it had the reverse effect from what he anticipated. Instead of stampeding the settlers into a mass exodus, it reinforced their determination to stand their ground.

Jim Jarrott's grieving widow, Mollie, struggled out of her sick bed, seized her late husband's torch, climbed into a buggy and rode to all the homesteader's tents, dugouts, and shacks. Her message: "Stay put!" Not only that, Mollie made sure that the six settlers who were the defendants in the upcoming law suits challenging their homestead claims were not left in the lurch. The law suits against them were dismissed.

One of Jarrott's first homesteaders, Mary Blankenship, summed up the settlers' reaction to Jim Jarrott's murder when she commented:

Instead of being scared off of our claims...we became more intent and closely allied in our fight for survival. The name Jim Jarrott became a legend among us, and his martyrdom served to spur us on. We were determined not to pull up stakes and retreat back to the East.[5]

Ida Lee Cowan, wife of another of Jarrott's settlers, added this:

Nothing daunted us...We came with the determination to stay, and we stayed.[6]

The tides of time were also in the process of turning in favor of the western bound, covered wagon immigrants. Back in Austin, the Texas capitol, a populist governor, James S. Hogg, was elected in 1891, in 1895, the Texas legislature enacted the homesteader friendly Four-Section Act, and in 1902 the Texas Supreme Court, in the *Ketner v. Rogan* case, outlawed the cattle king's favorite ploy of extending indefinitely their cheap leases on large blocks of state land. The flamboyant, early day Texas Panhandle lawyer, land promoter, and historian Judge James Hamlin wrote that the Four-Section Act, more than any other factor, brought about the settlement of West Texas, and "set off an influx of settlers fanning out through the large ranches in decrepit wagons, often containing their families, all their worldly possessions, and pulled by tired plow horses."[7]

Those pioneers may have been poor in worldly goods, but they were rich in energy, grit, determination, and boundless hope of staking off and claiming their share of the American dream. And endowing their descendants with a future enriched with opportunities for a better life.

In her memoirs recorded half a century later, Mary Blankenship reflected:

> The pioneer woman of the prairie soon sacrificed her femininity as she laid away her frills for the plain living, and took upon herself the yoke beside her husband as team mate and companion...Our day was from daylight till dark. But what a thrill to Andy and me to have been two of the few who blazed the trail for the multitudes that followed.[8]

Even though the geographical location in the Jarrott story is the same location that South Plains residents now occupy, Jarrott's story reveals a time in the past—and not so very many years ago—when life on the South Plains differed drastically from the present. Soon after Jarrott's death (only an eyeblink in the history of mankind) came the railroad, the automobile, the airplane, the space ship, and during the same time frame came the telegraph, the telephone, the radio, the motion pictures, the television, the internet. And on and on. Meanwhile, from yesterday's covered wagons creeping across the lonesome prairie the scene has shifted to today's life in the fast lane with shiny new, air-conditioned automobiles and trucks zipping along multi-lane highways. Never before in all the centuries of man's existence has life changed so drastically, so rapidly.

Consider the life of Wallace Blankenship, son of Andrew and Mary Blankenship. He was a six-month-old baby when he arrived on the South Plains in 1901, riding in a covered wagon as it labored slowly up the steep, narrow trail climbing the Caprock escarpment, yet he lived to witness a man setting foot on the moon. Moreover, Wallace's career spotlights an incredible leap into the future: the baby in the covered wagon to a first grader in an isolated one-room school on the prairie, to an electrical engineering student at Texas A&M college, to his establishment of the first motion picture theater on the South Plains, and then on to expanding his business so that at one time he owned a chain of thirty motion picture theaters in eleven area towns.[9]

Hostilities between the big ranchers and the homesteaders peaked after the assassination of J. W. Jarrott. It polarized the ranching and the homesteader communities. The bitterness continued for years. However, with time, the animosity began to dissipate. Shortly before her death in 1955, Mary Blankenship dictated her memoirs. She recalled, "In time our differences with the big ranchers dissolved, love overcame fear, and our tensions gave way to harmony. We came to understand and to believe that 'the West is for us and not against us.'"[10]

Mary Blankenship was the first woman among Jarrott's settlers to establish a home on the South Plains, and together with husband Andrew, they not only survived the hardships and rigors of pioneer life, but thrived, and over the years contributed much to the development of the South Plains. Andrew and Mary Blankenship donated the land for the first school in Hockley County. After the extension of the railroad from Lubbock, the Blankenships donated the land for the railroad right-of-way, the stock pens, and the section house at Ropesville. Andrew was instrumental in organizing a bank at Ropesville, and he served as one of its directors. He also aided in establishing the first cotton gin in Hockley County. In 1916, the Blankenships exchanged their horse and mule trading business for forty acres of land one mile northwest of downtown Lubbock. Six years later, in 1923, Texas Technological College was located along the southern boundary of this tract. Later the Blankenships developed the acreage into business units including the Town and Country Shopping Center.[11]

J. W. Jarrott's widow, Mollie, was another settler who made major contributions to the development of the South Plains. For seventeen years after her husband's murder, Mollie continued to occupy the land upon which she and J. W. Jarrott had filed. She operated it as a cattle ranch and expanded the ranch from the original four sections to a spread of sixteen sections where she pastured 400 head of registered Hereford cattle.

Mollie also engaged in businesses in Lubbock. She was a charter member of Lubbock's Business and Professional Women's Club. She also took an active role in promoting woman suffrage, was a leader in the prohibition movement, and served as president of both the League of Women Voters and the Woman's Christian Temperance Union. Three years after the murder of her husband, Mollie married a prominent Lubbock real estate developer, Monroe G. Abernathy. Both took an active role in the development of downtown Lubbock and constructed several commercial buildings. On one of the buildings that Mollie constructed, her friends affixed a bronze plaque bearing this legend: "Erected 1952 by Mollie D. and Monroe G. Abernathy as an example of their courage, vision and faith in the great South Plains of Texas."[12]

J. W. Jarrott's homestead seekers and their descendants weren't the only ones who made significant contributions to the development of the South Plains in later years. Some of the descendants of the large ranches also contributed. Perhaps the most outstanding of whom was Christine DeVitt, daughter of David DeVitt, owner of the Mallet Ranch. Back in 1902, DeVitt, together with the owners of the Lake-Tomb L7 Ranch registered a complaint against Texas General Land Office Commissioner Charles Rogan, charging him with unlawfully favoring J. W. Jarrott in claiming homesteads on "the Strip." When his complaint was denied DeVitt, in 1903, filed his own four-section claim on the Strip, located just west of Jarrott and his claimants. DeVitt proved up his claim, and that was where he located the headquarters of the sprawling Mallett Ranch.

DeVitt's daughter, Christine, enjoyed her times on the ranch. Unlike the other members of the DeVitt family, Christine looked forward to returning to her father's ranch each summer and taking full advantage of "the opportunity to improve her outdoor skills and horseback riding."[13]

In 1938, oil was discovered on the Mallet, and that first well turned out to be only the tip of a mighty iceberg of oil. By the early 1990s oil production from the Mallet would amount to nearly a billion barrels, and it has since continued. By the early 1980s, Christine DeVitt, who had never married and who owned one fourth of the minerals under the Mallett Ranch, had become a multimillionaire and was probably the wealthiest woman in Lubbock. She made many generous contributions to hospitals, colleges, and other charities; she became one of the city's greatest philanthropists. Among her beneficiaries were Texas Tech

University, Lubbock Christian University, South Plains College, and the Methodist Hospital School of Nursing, as well as others. Before her death in 1983, Christine had contributed more than two-and-one-half million dollars to Texas Tech University alone. In addition, she endowed the Ranching Heritage Center located on the Texas Tech campus with more than a million dollars.[14] Later, Christine DeVitt's younger sister, Helen DeVitt Jones, made large donations to various charities including three and a half million dollars to the West Texas Museum Association and other departments and colleges in the Texas Tech University complex.[15]

The South Plains of Llano Estacado with the city of Lubbock as its hub was a vastly different place by 2016 than it had been slightly more than a century earlier when J. W. Jarrott and his homestead seekers arrived in covered wagons. Looking back, Mollie reflected:

> There's never been anybody who did more for the settlement of this country than Mr. Jarrott, and he gave his life for it.[16]

There are no last chapters in history. The assassin's bullet may have ended J. W. Jarrott's life, but it did not end his story. It continues.

Mollie Abernathy died in Lubbock, Texas, in 1960 at age ninety-four.[17]

Figure 32. Tombstone of Jarrott and his father G. (Dr. Gardner) Jarrott

(Author's collection.)
Lubbock Municipal Cemetery

Appendix

Chronicle of the Timeline

Chronicle of the timeline of the (1)"First-Chair" battle for purchase of the four school sections; (2) the "deed-shuffle" scam for the four railroad sections; (3) and the assassination of J. W. Jarrott.

January 27, 1902

Deacon Jim Miller first appears on the Terry County scene. He witnesses and notarizes a deed from Z. T. Joiner conveying the four checker-boarded railroad sections to D. J. Howard. Howard pays Joiner $896 cash for the four sections (2,560 acres).

February 1902

Texas General Land office announces that when Pap Brownfield's lease on the four school sections expires next year the land would be sold pursuant to the Texas "Four-Sections Act" for $1 an acre to the prospective buyer who held "first chair" at the county clerk's office on the morning of February 17, 1903.

March 1902

Pap Brownfield's son, A. M. "Dick" Brownfield, arrives in a covered wagon with his wife and daughter. Pap assigns his lease on the four checker-boarded school sections that are interlocked with Howard's four checker-boarded railroad sections. Dick builds a house on one of the leased school sections. These are the four school sections that are to be sold by the state to the "first chair" holders next February 17, 1903.

August 27, 1902

Deacon Jim Miller assassinates J. W. Jarrott in Terry County approximately fifteen miles northeast of the two four-section tracts Brownfield and Howard are contesting.

October 1902

Dick Brownfield sends representatives to the back door of the clerk's office and begins contesting for the "first chair" position to buy the four school sections—four months before the clerk was to accept applications on February 17, 1903. Howard then responds by sending his men (his two grown sons) to contest the "first-chair" position.

January 23, 1903

Deacon Jim Miller reappears and persuades D. J. Howard to sign a deed conveying to him the four railroad sections Howard had acquired a year earlier from Z. T. Joiner. No cash down. The only consideration is an assignment by Miller to Howard of a $3,900 promissory note payable to Miller and executed by T. J. Coggin, the man who claims to be a banker from Merkel, Texas. The note is collateralized by a large tract of land Coggin supposedly owned in East Texas. The ninety-day promissory note is payable in full on March 31, 1903. But, in the Howard-to-Miller deed, no lien is reserved by Howard on his four railroad sections in order to guarantee payment of the Coggin note or to permit recovery by Howard of title to his land in the event Coggin defaults.

January 30, 1903

One week after he acquires title to Howard's four railroad sections, Miller sells the land to a Fort Worth banker named W. H. Fisher. The deed recites that the alleged purchase price for the land is $4,100. Cash. The banker does not agree to guarantee payment of Coggin's $3,900 note Miller assigned to Howard and no lien is reserved to permit Howard to foreclose and recover his land in the event Coggin defaults.

February 17, 1903

Dick Brownfield wins the battle for "first chair" at the county clerk's office and buys the four school sections for $1.00 per acre to be paid out over forty years at three percent interest.

March 7, 1903

Fort Worth banker W. H. Fisher sells the four railroad sections he had just acquired from Jim Miller to A. M. "Dick" Brownfield for $800 cash. Again, there is no provision in Fisher's deed requiring Dick Brownfield to guarantee payment of Coggin's promissory note or any lien reserved to allow foreclosure on the land conveyed if Coggin defaults on payment of his $3,900 note. With Dick Brownfield's purchase of these four railroad sections from banker W. J. Fisher, together with his purchase of the four interlocking school sections he had just bought from the state on February 17, 1903, the entire interlocking eight-section block at the center of Terry County is now owned by Dick Brownfield. And D. J. Howard now owns nary an acre.

March 31, 1903

The $3,900 Coggin note Miller had assigned to D. J. Howard becomes due in full. Coggin defaults. Since neither Miller nor banker Fisher nor Dick Brownfield had guaranteed payment of T. J. Coggin's note—the $3,900 note that Jim Miller had assigned to Howard—and since Howard had failed to reserve a lien on his land providing for recovery of his land by a foreclosure if Coggin defaulted, Howard must look for payment to the alleged "Merkel banker," T. J. Coggin. Trouble is, Coggin had signed that $3,900 note and is not a banker. Not in Merkel nor anywhere else. What Coggin really is, is a bosom buddy of Jim Miller. And the lien on that large block of East Texas land that Coggin supposedly owned, that was also assigned by Miller to Howard as collateral for payment of the note? Well, as it turned out, that was also worthless. It was a very large swamp. To which Coggin had no title.

End Result

Dick Brownfield with assistance and advice from his father, M. V. "Pap" Brownfield, now owns all eight interlocking sections of land: four school sections and four railroad sections in Terry County, Texas, including the section where the county seat town of Brownfield is now located.

D. J. Howard owns nary an acre.

Deacon Jim Miller departs Terry County, his saddlebags stuffed full of cash, and heads for home back in Fort Worth, well paid for his dual roles as hitman and conman: hitman for successfully assassinating J. W. Jarrott, leader of the nesters, and conman for devising and executing the master scam that swindled D. J. Howard out of his four railroad sections of land.

J. W. "Jim" Jarrott, R.I.P.; martyr of the nesters' cause: "He gave his life for it."

Endnotes

Preface

1. A biography as told to J. Evetts Haley and William Curry Holden, *The Flamboyant Judge: James D. Hamlin* (Canyon, Texas: Palo Duro Press, 1972), 11-12.

2. Don Graham, "Notes from Texas," *On Writing in the Lone Star State* (Fort Worth: TCU Press, 2008), 59.

Chapter One

1. Seymour V. Conner, ed., *The West Is for Us: The Reminiscences of Mary Blankenship* (Lubbock: West Texas Museum Association Journal, 1958), 2: 25-26.

2. The Reminiscences of Mary Blankenship, 26.

3. Ibid., 26.

4. Ibid.

5. Ibid., 27.

6. Ibid., 25, 31.

7. Ibid., 37; and from Jo Ella Powell Exley, ed., *Texas Tears and Texas Sunshine: Voices of Frontier Women* (College Station: Texas A&M University Press, 1985), 243-255; and Roy Sylvan Dunn, "Blankenship, A. W. and Mary," Seymour V. Conner, ed., *Builders of the Southwest* (Lubbock: Southwest Collection, Texas Technological College, 1959), 18-22. Also see Louis Fairchild, *The Lonesome Plains: Death and Revival on an American Frontier* (College Station: Texas A&M University Press, 2002).

CHAPTER TWO

1. John Miller Morris, *El Llano Estacado: Exploration and Imagination on the High Plains of Texas and New Mexico, 1530-1860* (Austin: Texas State Historical Association, 1997), 1-3; Art Leatherwood, "Llano Estacado," *The New Handbook of Texas* (Austin: Texas Historical Society, 1996), 4, 250-252; Paul H. Carlson, "100 Years Ago on the Llano Estacado," *Llano Estacado Heritage* 5 (Summer 1975). Also see Shelley Armitage, *Walking the Llano: A Texas Memoir of Place* (Norman: University of Oklahoma, 2016), 75.

2. Edwin James, "Account of an Expedition from Pittsburgh to the Rocky Mountains, Performed in the Years 1819 and 20...under the Command of Major Stephen H. Long" in *Early Western Travels*, ed. R. G. Thwaites (Cleveland, Ohio: Arthur H. Clark, 1905), 90, 95; Morris, *El Llano Estacado*, 202-204. Broadus Spivey and Jesse Sublett, *Broke Not Broken: Homer Maxey's Texas Bank War* (Lubbock: Texas Tech University Press, 2014), 20-22; Leatherwood, "Llano Estacado," *The New Handbook of Texas*, 4, 250-252.

3. Randolph B. Marcy, letter from the Secretary of War George W. Crawford, Feb. 21, 1850, "Route from Fort Smith to Santa Fe," H. Exec. Doc. 45, 31st Cong., 1st Sess, p. 41; Morris, *El Llano Estacado*, 260-261. Paul H. Carlson, *Amarillo: The Story of a Western Town* (Lubbock: Texas Tech University Press, 2006), 14-15; Ernest R. Archambeau, "The Fort Smith-Santa Fe Trail Along the Canadian River in Texas," *Panhandle-Plains Historical Review* 27 (1954), 1-26; Broadus Spivey and Jesse Sublett, *Broke Not Broken: Homer Maxey's Texas Bank War* (Lubbock: Texas Tech University Press, 2014), 20-22; Leatherwood, "Llano Estacado," *The New Handbook of Texas*, 4:250-252. In Texas, the twenty northern counties of West Texas—the Panhandle—is designated as the "North Plains" and the adjoining seventeen southern counties as the "South Plains." See Louis Fairchild, *The Lonesome Plains: Death and Revival on an American Frontier* (College Station: Texas A&M University Press, 2002), 213n2.

4. See Leatherwood, "Llano Estacado," *The New Handbook of Texas*, 4, 251, and sources cited thereafter, page 252; and Armitage, *Walking the Llano: A Texas Memoir of Place*, 75, 142.

5. J. Evetts Haley, *Charles Goodnight: Cowman and Plainsman* (Norman: University of Oklahoma Press, 1949), 276, 294; Rupert N. Richardson, *Texas: The Lone Star State* (New York: Prentice-Hall, 1943), 310.

6. J. Evetts Haley, *The XIT Ranch of Texas and the Early Days of Llano Estacado* (Norman: University of Oklahoma Press, 1967), 49-57; Lewis Nordyke, *Cattle Empire: The Fabulous Story of the 3,000,000 Acre XIT* (New York: William Morrow, 1949), 159-173.

7. Hans Peter Nicolson Gammell, comp. *Laws of the State of Texas*, 1822-1897; Vol. 10, H. B. No. 30, 25th Legislature (Austin: Gammel, 1898), 1480; Jeanne Dibrell, *The New Handbook of Texas*, "Four-Sections Act" (Austin: Texas State Historical Association, 1996), 2:1138.

8. *James D. Hamlin, The Flamboyant Judge: The Story of Amarillo and the Development of the Great Ranches of the Texas Panhandle,* an autobiography as told to J. Evetts Haley and William Curry Holden (Canyon, TX: Palo Duro Press, 1972), 11-12.

9. David J. Murrah, *Oil, Taxes, and Cats: A History of the DeVitt Family and the Mallet Ranch* (Lubbock: Texas Tech University Press, 1994), 35-36.

Chapter Three

1. Seymour V. Conner, ed., *The West Is for Us: The Reminiscences of Mary A. Blankenship* (Lubbock: West Texas Museum Association, 1958), V. 2; 26-27; Fairchild, *The Lonesome Plains: Death and Revival on an American Frontier*, 13.

2. Connor, *The West Is for Us, The Reminiscences of Mary Blankenship*, 34; Lillian Brasher, *Hockley County, 1921-1971* (Canyon, TX: Staked Plains Press, 19__), 52.

3. Connor, *The West Is for Us, The Reminiscences of Mary Blankenship*, 1-24; Jo Ella Powell Exley, ed., *Texas Tears and Texas Sunshine: Voices of Frontier Women* (College Station: Texas A&M University Press, 1985), 241-255; Seymour V. Connor, ed., *Builders of the Southwest: A. W. and Mary Blankenship*, by Roy Sylvan Dunn (Lubbock: Southwest Collections, Texas Technological College, 1959), 18-21.

4. Connor, *The West Is for Us: The Reminiscences of Mary Blankenship*, 1-24; Jo Ella Powell Exley, ed., *Texas Tears and Texas Sunshine: Voices of Frontier Women*, 241-255; Seymour V. Conner, ed., *Builders of the Southwest: A. W. and Mary Blankenship*, by Roy Sylvan Dunn, 18-21.

5. Exley, *Texas Tears and Texas Sunshine*, 243.

6. Connor, *The West Is for Us: The Reminiscences of Mary Blankenship*, 2

CHAPTER FOUR

1. Chuck Lanehart, "A History Mystery: Who Shot J. W.?" *Voice for the Defense* magazine, May 2011, Vol. 4, No. 4: 26-33. Also see Yvonne Spence Perkins and Judy Womack, *Death on the Plains: The Murder of Jim Jarrott* (Private Printing, 2010, available at Southwest Collection Library, Texas Tech University, Lubbock, Texas.)

2. June M. Steele, "Mollie Abernathy: Rancher of the South Plains, 1900-1909," (Lubbock: *West Texas Historical Association*, 1999), Vol. LXXV: 102.

3. A. C. Greene, *Sketches from the Five States of Texas* (College Station: Texas A&M University Press, 1998), 193.

4. Seymour V. Conner, ed., *Builders of the Southwest: Mollie B. Abernathy* (Lubbock: Southwest Collection Library, Texas Technological College, 1959), 3-5; Seymour V. Conner, "Mollie Wylie Abernathy," *The New Handbook of Texas* (Austin: Texas State Historical Association, 1996), 1: 7; *Lubbock Avalanche-Journal*, June 5, 1960.

5. Lanehart, *Voice for the Defense*, 26.

6. Lawrence A. Landis, "Lanham, Samuel Willis Tucker," *The New Handbook of Texas* (Austin: Texas State Historical Commission, 1996), 4:69.

7. Personnel File of the Texas State Government with Sketches of Distinguished Texans, Embracing The Executive and Staff, Heads of the Departments, United States Senators and Representatives, Members of the Twentieth Legislature, Compiled and Published by L. E. Daniel, (Austin: Press of the City Print Company, 1887), J. W. Jarrott, p. 142.

8. Tape One of tape-recorded interview of Mollie and Monroe Abernathy by Seymour V. Conner, June 4 and 7, 1956, Southwest Collection, Texas Tech University, Lubbock, Texas.

9. Wayne Alvord, "T. L. Nugent: Texas Populist," *Southwestern Historical Quarterly* (Austin: Texas State Historical Commission, July 1953), 57; Worth Robert Miller, "Nugent, Thomas Lewis," *The New Handbook of Texas* (Austin: Texas State Historical Commission, 1996), 4:1075. See also Sherri Knight, *Vigilantes to Verdicts: Stories from a Texas District Court* (Stephenville, Texas: Jacobus Books, 2009), 161, 163-65, 176, 191.

10. Tape One of Mollie and Monroe Abernathy interview.

11. William N. Tood IV and Gerald Knape, "Rogan, Charles," *The New Handbook of Texas* (Austin: Texas State Historical Commission, 1996), 5:661.

12. Report and Procedures of the [Texas] State Legislative Investigating Committee, investigating charges leveled against [Texas] State General Land Office; Austin, Texas May 17, 1902; p. 113-115. Google Books, http:/books.google.com/books?id. The committee was investigating a complaint filed by Lubbock County officials: W. D. Crum, County Judge; F. L. Phenix, Comr. Pre. No. One; R. C. Burns, Comr. Pre. No. Two; J. B. Mobley, Clerk, County Courts; J. D. Caldwell, County Treasurer; J. C. Bowlen, Tax Assessor; and Easton Wolfforth, sheriff. The complaint alleged that GLO Commissioner Rogan unfairly favored his friend J. W.

Jarrott in the sale of school lands in Hockley County, Texas, on April 24, 1902, to "J. W. Jarrott and others represented by him." Rogan, in his answer, did disclose that J. W. Jarrott had deposited with the GLO the sum of $500 to enable the employment of Mark Ragsdale to begin his survey of the unsurveyed strip of land and that the 1902 Texas Legislature had appropriated $3,000 to complete the survey.

13. Tape One of Mollie and Monroe Abernathy interview; June M. Steele, "Mollie Abernathy, Rancher of the South Plains, 1900-1919," *West Texas Historical Association Yearbook*, 1999), LXIV: 102.

14. Report of the State Legislative Investigating Committee, 113-115. Also see William C. Billingsley, "The Strip," *Recollections from the Heart of Hockley County* (Dallas: Taylor Publishing Company, 1986), 201-202; and *The Hockley County Herald*, March 4, 1938.

15. Jo Ella Powell Exley, *Texas Tears and Texas Sunshine*, 245; Seymour V. Conner, ed., *The West Is for Us: The Reminiscences of Mary A. Blankenship*, 1-43.

CHAPTER FIVE

1. Fairchild, *The Lonesome Plains*, xv.

2. Conner, *The West Is for Us: The Reminiscences of Mary A. Blankenship*, 37; Exley, *Texas Tears and Texas Sunshine*, 248.

3. Orville R. Watkins, *Hockley County: From Cattle Ranches to Farms* (Abilene, TX: West Texas Historical Association Yearbook, 1941), 53.

4. Conner, *The West Is for Us*, 23, 27; Fairchild, *The Lonesome Plains*, 5; Mrs. Ida Lee Cowan, "Early Days on the Plains," *The Lubbock Morning Avalanche*, June 13, 1924.

5. Conner, *The West Is for Us*, 30.

6. Exley, *Texas Tears and Texas Sunshine*, 248; June M. Steele, *Mollie M. Abernathy: Rancher of the South Plains, 1900-1919* (Lubbock: West Texas Historical Association Yearbook, 1999), 102.

7. Conner, *The West Is for Us*, 36.

8. Conner, *The West Is for Us*, 70; Exley, *Texas Tears and Texas Sunshine*, 252; Fairchild, *The Lonesome Plains*, 30.

9. Conner, *The West Is for Us*, 41; Exley, *Texas Tears and Texas Sunshine*, 248;

10. Conner, *The West Is for Us*, 80; Fairchild, *The Lonesome Plains*, 50.

11. Riley Moffat, *Population of Western U.S. Cities and Towns, 1850-1900* (Lanham, MD: Scarecrow Press, 1996), 87. This census shows 117 inhabitants in the town of Lubbock. The 1900 U.S. Census shows 293 inhabitants in the county of Lubbock. See Chapter Two, page 2; supra.

12. James H. Nunn Sr., interview by Omah Ryan, 1937, p. 3-5, Research Center, Panhandle-Plains Museum, Canyon, Texas; Fairchild, *The Lonesome Plains*, 27, 225n3.

13. Exley, *Texas Tears and Texas Sunshine*, 251.

14. Conner, *The West Is for Us*, 37.

15. Exley, *Texas Tears and Texas Sunshine*, 250.

16. Fairchild, *The Lonesome Plains*, 147-150.

17. Ibid.

Chapter Six

1. Charles Rogan, Report of State Legislative Investigating Committee, 113-115.

2. Ibid.

3. Ibid.

4. F. L. Dole, "The West Made Habitable by Windmills," *The Cattleman* magazine, 19 (October 1932), 14; Leland Turner, "Grassland Beef Factories: Frontier Cattle Raisers in Northwest Texas and the Queensland Outback," *Panhandle-Plains Historical Review,* Vol. LXXXVI (2015), 7-30; Walter Prescott Webb, *The Great Plains* (New York: Gosset & Dunlap, 1931), 333-348.

5. Gammel, *Laws of State of Texas,* (1895 as amended 1897), 10:63-77), *General Laws of Texas,* 793-807; David J. Murrah, *C. C. Slaughter: Rancher, Banker, Baptist* (Austin: University of Texas Press, 1981), 84; J. Evetts Haley, *Charles Goodnight: Cowman and Plainsman* (Boston: Houghton Mifflin, 1936), 401; Paul H. Carlson, *Empire Builder in the Texas Panhandle: William Henry Bush* (College Station: Texas A&M University Press, 1996), 105.

6. *Ketner v. Rogan,* et al, 95 Tex.Ct.App. 559, 68 S.W. 774 (Tex. Sup. Ct., 1902); Paul H. Carlson, *Amarillo: The Story of a Western Town* (Lubbock: Texas Tech University, 2006), 62-64; *Dallas Morning News,* May 20, 1902, "Suit Involving Land Lease: Interesting Question In Case Pending Before Supreme Court; *Fort Worth Morning Register,* June 10, 1902, "Can Now Get Texas Homes: Supreme Court Decides in Favor of Homesteader."

7. J. A. Rickards, "South Plains Land Rushes," (Canyon, TX: *Panhandle-Plains Historical Review* V. II (1929), 98-103; R. D. Holt, "School Land Rushes in West Texas" (Abilene, TX: *The West Texas Historical Association* V. X (1934), 42-57; Orville R. Watkins, "Hockley County: From Cattle Ranches To Farmers" (Abilene, TX: *West Texas Historical Association* V. XVII (1941), 44-70; Leland K. Turner, "The West Texas Plains," Paul H. Carlson and Bruce A. Glasrud, *West Texas: A History of the Giant Side of the State* (Norman: University of Oklahoma Press, 2014), 48-52.

Chapter Seven

1. Mollie Jarrott Monroe in a tape-recorded interview of Mollie and Monroe Abernathy by Seymour V. Conner (Lubbock, Texas: June 3, 1956), Southwest Collections Library, Texas Tech University.

2. Seymour V. Conner, ed., "The West Is for Us: The Reminiscences of Mary A. Blankenship," *The Museum Journal* (Lubbock: West Texas Museum Association, 1958), Vol. 2, pgs. 41-43.

3. Ibid.; Glenn Shirley, *Shotgun for Hire: The Story of "Deacon" Jim Miller* (Norman: University of Oklahoma Press, 1970), 57; Terry County Historical Survey, *Early Settlers of Terry County: A History of Terry County, Texas* (Hereford, Texas: Pioneer Book Publishers, Inc., 1968), 50-51.

4. Memoirs of Anna Laura Cowan Daniels (daughter of Lee Cowan), and memoirs of Lee Cowan, "Pioneers and Primrose School," interview notes obtained by John and Bette Hope, Levelland, Texas. See also Ronnie and Sandra McNabb, *Ropes Remembers* (Ropesville, Texas: private printing by Nunn Printing Co., 1974). Lee Cowan was one of the community leaders in what is now known as the village of Ropesville. Lee Cowan, Andrew Blankenship, and a Mr. Baker were the trustees of the first school in the community—the school was named Primrose. Lee Cowan was also instrumental in organizing the First Baptist Church in the community and was the first and only deacon for a number of years. (His wife, Rebecca, played the organ for services.) Lee was also the unofficial community doctor, performing many services from pulling teeth to administering drugs such as Black Draught Tea for a laxative, Calamia for high fever, and a homemade mix for cough syrup. Rebecca, served as midwife in delivering babies for neighboring women. They never charged a fee for their services, and the weather was never too bad nor the distance too far for Rebecca to travel across the prairie to deliver a baby or for Lee to render emergency medical services. When Hockley County was organized in 1921, Lee was elected as one of the first County Commissioners. He was re-elected, and served two terms.

Lee and Rebecca Cowan were the parents of ten children. John Hope, *Texas' Last Frontier Ranch Heritage, 2011 Tour Guide*, 59-60.

5. Wayne Gard, "Fence Cutting," *The New Handbook of Texas* (Austin: Texas State Historical Association, 1996), Vol. 2, 976. In 1884 the Texas Legislature enacted the fence-cutting statute making it a felony criminal offense to cut another's fence—one to five years in the penitentiary. Paul Burka, "The Open Range R.I.P., 1866-1884," *Texas Monthly* magazine, January 1986, 43.

6. Max Coleman, "Who Killed This Man," *Frontier Times* magazine, Vol. 8, No. 12, September 1931; Lanehart, "A History Mystery: Who Shot J. W.?," *Voice for the Defense* magazine, May 2011, Vol. 4, No. 4, 28-29.

7. John Hope, "Jim Jarrott and The Strip," *Texas' Last Frontier Ranch Heritage, 2010 Tour Guide* (Levelland: Hockley and Cochran County Historical Commissions), 53. For background information on Oliver C. "Bird" Rose, see Ike Blassingame, *Dakota Cowboy: My Life in the Old Days* (New York: G. P. Putman's Sons, 1958), 218-24.

8. Seymour V. Conner, tape recorded interview of Mollie Monroe, supra.

9. Ibid.; Glenn Shirley, *Shotgun for Hire,* 42.

10. Ronnie and Sandra McNabb, *Ropes Remembers,* supra, 6.

11. Monroe Abernathy letter to Judge Frost Woodhull, March 27, 1933 (Lubbock: Southwest Collection Library, folders on Mollie and Monroe Abernathy.)

12. Monroe Abernathy letter to Judge Frost Woodhull, March 27, 1933, supra; Lanehart, "A History Mystery: Who Shot J. W.?" supra.

13. *Fort Worth Star-Telegram*, "Murder in West Texas," September 4, 1902.

14. Ronnie and Sandra McNabb, *Ropes Remembers,* 6.

15. Seymour V. Conner, tape recording interview of Mollie and Monroe Abernathy, supra.

16. Lanehart, "A History Mystery: Who Shot J. W.?," 28.

17. Monroe Abernathy letter to Judge Frost Woodhull, March 27, 1933 (Lubbock: Southwest Collections Library, folders on Mollie and Monroe Abernathy.)

18. David J. Murrah, *Oil, Taxes, and Cats: History of the DeVitt Family and the Mallet Ranch* (Lubbock: Texas Tech University Press, 1994), 34-35.

19. Seymour V. Conner, "The West Is for Us: The Reminiscences of Mary A. Blankenship," 42; Jo Ella Powell Exley, *Texas Tears and Texas Sunshine* (College Station: Texas A&M University Press, 1985), 249.

20. Seymour V. Conner, Mollie Abernathy interview; John Hope, *Texas' Last Frontier, Ranch Heritage, 2011 Tour Guide*, 14.

21. Mrs. Ida Lee Cowan "Early Days on the Plains," *Lubbock Morning Avalanche*, January 13, 1924, reprinted in the March 15, 1999 edition of the *Lubbock Avalanche-Journal.*

22. Seymour V. Conner, "The West Is for Us: Reminiscences of Mary A. Blankenship," 43; Exley, *Texas Tears and Texas Sunshine*, 249; Murrah, *Oil, Taxes, and Cats: History of the DeVitt Family and the Mallet Ranch*, 34-35.

23. John Hope, *Texas' Last Frontier Ranch Heritage, 2011 Tour Guide*, 14.

24. *J. W. Barrington v. Noah Bell*, Cause No. 84 in the District Court of Martin County, Texas.

25. Walter Dibrell, "Smith, William Robert," *The New Handbook of Texas* (Austin: Texas State Historical Association, 1996), Vol. 5, 1111.

26. Seymour V. Conner, Mollie Abernathy interview tape, supra.

27. David J. Murrah, *Oil, Taxes, and Cats*, 36; Seymour V. Conner, Mollie Abernathy tape.

28. Seymour V. Conner, Mollie Abernathy tape.

29. Ibid.

30. Ibid.

31. Indictments returned by the Lubbock County grand jury in the 50th Judicial District Court on October 3, 1903, in the J. W. Jarrott murder investigation: Cause No. 67, *State v. B. F. Nix* (perjury); Cause No. 68, *State v. B. F. Nix* (murder); Cause No. 69, *State v. J. W. Barrington* (murder); Cause No. 70, *State v. Morgan Bellow* (murder); Cause No. 71, *State v. B. G. Glaser* (murder). Although the murder of Jarrott occurred in Hockley County, the county had a population of only forty-four at that time and was not an organized county. Therefore at that time it was attached to Lubbock County, an organized county, for judicial purposes, and that is where the indictments were returned.

32. Bail bondsman Frank Wheelock would later distinguish himself by becoming, in 1909, the first mayor of the city of Lubbock, and a school in Lubbock would later be named in his honor. However, prior to all of that, in 1891, Frank Wheelock also distinguished himself by becoming the first person in the history of Lubbock County to be indicted for a felony crime—actually two felony crimes: fence-cutting and cattle theft. The charges, however, were later dismissed. Lanehart, "A History Mystery: Who Shot J. W. ?", 34.

33. The Lubbock County grand jury indictments for the murder and perjury of the four defendants that had been transferred to Floydada in Floyd County on a change of venue order were later, on May 20, 1905, and September 26, 1905, dismissed on grounds of insufficient evidence by joint motion of the prosecution and defense in Cause Nos. 250 and 251 in the Floyd County District Court.

34. Seymour V. Connor, Mollie Abernathy interview tape, supra.

CHAPTER EIGHT

1. David J. Murrah, *Oil, Taxes, and Cats: A History of the DeVitt Family and the Mallet Ranch* (Lubbock: Texas Tech University Press), 1994, 35.

2. Glenn Shirley, *Shotgun for Hire: The Story of "Deacon" Jim Miller* (Norman: University of Oklahoma Press, 1970), 8-10.

3. Ibid.

4. Ibid.; C. L. Sonnichsen, *Texas Feuds: "Vengeance Is Mine!" Saith the Lord, But in Texas He Has Always had Plenty of Help!* (Albuquerque: University of New Mexico Press, 1957), 204; William A Keleher, *The Fabulous Frontier* (Santa Fe: The Rydal Press, 1942), 78-79; Bill C. James, *Jim Miller: The Untold Story of a Texas Badman* (Wolfe City, TX: Henington Publishing Company, 1989), 1-2; Dee Harkey, *Mean as Hell: The Life of a New Mexico Lawman* (Santa Fe: Ancient City Press, 1989), 175.5

5. *James B. Miller v. State of Texas*, Cause No. 3283, 18 Tex.Ct.Crim.App. 232, May 20, 1885.

6. Shirley, *Shotgun for Hire*, 13; James, *Jim Miller: The Untold Story of a Texas Badman*, 4.

7. Shirley, *Shotgun for Hire*, 20.

8. Ibid., 25-26.

9. Ibid., 31-33.

10. Ibid., 34; James, *Jim Miller: The Untold Story of a Texas Badman*, 7-8.

11. Shirley, *Shotgun for Hire*, 41-44; James, *Jim Miller: The Untold Story of a Texas Badman*, 8-9.

12. Harkey, *Mean as Hell*, 176-177.

13. Shirley, *Shotgun for Hire*, 47-49; Sonnichsen, *Texas Feuds*, 207; James, *Jim Miller: The Untold Story of a Texas Badman*, 12. Official court records of the 91st Judicial District Court of Eastland County, Texas, reveal that the Reeves County, Texas, indictment of James B. Miller for the murder of G. A. "Bud" Frazer was transferred to the Eastland County District Court in March 1897; that the first murder trial (which ended in a hung jury mistrial) was held in June 1897; and that his third trial (which ended in an acquittal) was concluded in January 1899.

14. James, *Jim Miller*, 65; Shirley, *Shotgun for Hire*, 49.

15. Shirley, *Shotgun for Hire*, 49.

16. Harkey, *Mean as Hell: The Life of a New Mexico Lawman*, 175; Sonnichsen, *Texas Feuds*, 208; Keleher, *The Fabulous Frontier*, 78-79.

17. Shirley, *Shotgun for Hire*, 13; James, *Jim Miller*, 4.

18. Harkey, *Mean as Hell*, 179-180; James, *Jim Miller*, 25-26; Sonnichsen, *Texas Feuds*, 207.

19. Shirley, *Shotgun for Hire*, 49-52; James, *Jim Miller*, 25-28.

20. Ibid.

21. Ibid.

22. Shirley, *Shotgun for Hire*, 50; James, *Jim Miller*, 27-28.

23. *Miller v. State of Texas*, 43 Tex.Ct.Crim.App. 367; 65 S.W. 908, 1901.

24. Harkey, *Mean as Hell*, 178; Sonnichsen, *Texas Feuds*, 208; James, *Jim Miller*, 28.

25. Harkey, *Mean as Hell*, 178-179; James, *Jim Miller*, 28; Shirley, *Shotgun for Hire*, 49-52.

26. Ibid.

27. Letter dated March 23, 1933, from [former U.S. Marshal] Jack Abernathy to M.G. [Monroe] Abernathy, and letter dated March 27, 1933, from Monroe Abernathy to Judge Frost Woohull, James W. Jarrott Reference File, and folder on Mollie Abernathy and Monroe Abernathy, Southwest Collections Library, Texas Tech University, Lubbock, Texas.

28. Ibid.

29. Ibid.

30. The story of the killing of Frank Fore and the murder trial in Fort Worth is taken from Shirley, *Shotgun for Hire*, 59-60; James, *Jim Miller*, 29-30; Harkey, *Mean as Hell*, 179; newspaper stories from the *Fort Worth*

Record and the *Fort Worth Star-Telegram* from the shooting on March 10, 1904, and through the two-month murder trial ending on May 5, 1906, and court documents filed in the Frank Fore murder case: *State of Texas v. J. B. Miller*, Cause No. 16,869 in the 48th Judicial District Court of Tarrant County, Texas.

31. Shirley, *Shotgun for Hire*, 72-73.

32. John R. Abernathy, *Catch 'em Alive Jack: The Life and Adventures of an American Pioneer* (New York: Association Press, 1936). Also see, Bill Neal, *From Guns to Gavels: How Justice Grew Up in the Outlaw West* (Lubbock: Texas Tech University Press, 2008), 116-118.

33. Letter dated March 23, 1933, from Jack Abernathy to M. G. [Monroe] Abernathy; supra. Shirley, *Shotgun for Hire*, 72-73.

34. Shirley, *Shotgun for Hire*, 73.

35. Mark Lee Gardner, *To Hell on a Fast Horse: Billy the Kid, Pat Garrett, and the Epic Chase to Justice in the Old West* (New York: HarperCollins Publishers, 2010), 228-242; Shirley, *Shotgun for Hire*, 74-91; Sonnichsen, *Texas Feuds*, 208; *New Mexico Sentinel*, April 23, 1939.

36. Gardner, *To Hell on a Fast Horse*, 240.

37. Ibid., 232.

38. Ibid., 236.

39. Compare: Gardner, *To Hell on a Fast Horse*, 241-242, with Sonnichsen, *Texas Feuds*, 208-209; Shirley, *Shotgun for Hire*, 74-87; with Harkey, *Mean as Hell*, 183-189; with James, *Jim Miller*, 36-42; and with Ellis Lindsey, "Did Miller Kill Pat Garret?", *Wild West* magazine, October 2011, 47; and with Leon C. Metz, *Pat Garrett: The Story of a Western Lawman* (Norman: University of Oklahoma Press, 1974), 292-304; and with Chuck Lanehart, "A History Mystery: Who Shot J. W. Jarrott?" *Voice of the Defense*, 30-33; and with, Letter dated March 27, 1933, from Monroe Abernathy to Judge Frost Woodhull, supra.

40. *The Shawnee Daily Herald,* July 18, 1905; Shirley, *Shotgun for Hire,* 100.

41. Shirley, *Shotgun for Hire,* 105-106.

42. Howard K. Berry, *He Made It Safe to Murder: The Life of Moman Pruiett* (Oklahoma City: Oklahoma Heritage Association, 2001); Moman Pruiett, *Criminal Lawyer* (Oklahoma City: Harlow Publishing Corporation, 1944); Shirley, *Shotgun for Hire,* 96-97.

43. Shirley, *Shotgun for Hire,* 115.

44. Ibid.

45. The lynching of Jim Miller was also reported in *The Dallas Morning News,* April 20, 1909, and in *The Galveston News,* April 20, 1909, and in *The Ada [Oklahoma] Weekly News,* April 22, 1909.

46. Letter from Monroe Abernathy to Judge Frost Woohull dated March 29, 1933, supra.

47. Ibid.; Murrah, *Oil, Taxes, and Cats,* 35-36; Also see Terry County Historical Commission, "Notorious Badman 'Deacon' Jim Miller," *Terry County Texas* (Clanton, AL: Heritage Publishing Consultants, 2002), 54-55; and Terry County Historical Survey Committee, "J. W. Jarrott," in *Early Settlers of Terry: A History of Terry County, Texas* (Hereford, TX: Pioneer Book Publishers, 1968), 49-54.

CHAPTER NINE

1. Mrs. Roy Wingered, "M. V. Brownfield's Colorful Career Is Recollected by Kin," *Terry County Herald,* December 3, 1937; Kyle Buckner, "History of Terry County," Master's thesis, Texas Technological College, Lubbock, Texas, 1943; Glen H. Mitchell, "Three Major Crises in the Life of Terry County," Master's thesis, Texas Technological College, Lubbock, Texas, 1957.

2. Ronnie and Sandra McNabb, *Ropes Remembers* (private publisher, 1974), 5-6.

3. Indictments returned by the Lubbock County grand jury on October 3, 1903, in the J. W. Jarrott murder investigation: Cause No. 67, *State v. B. F. Nix* (perjury); Cause No. 68, *State v. B. F. Nix* (murder); Cause No. 69, *State v. J. W. Barrington* (murder); Cause No. 70, *State v. Morgan Bellow* (murder); Cause No. 71, *State v. B. G. Glaser* (murder). All indictments were filed in the 50th Judicial District Court of Lubbock County. Although the murder of Jarrott occurred in Hockley County, that county had a population of only forty-four at that time and was not an organized county. Therefore it was attached to Lubbock County, an organized county for judicial purposes.

Those Lubbock County indictments were transferred to Floydada in Floyd County on a change of venue order but later, on September 26, 1905, were dismissed on grounds of insufficient evidence by joint motion of the prosecution and defense in Cause Nos. 250 and 251 in the Floyd County District Court. See also *Dallas Morning News*, May 14, 1905.

4. Letter dated March 23, 1933, from [former U.S. Marshal] Jack Abernathy to M. G. [Monroe] Abernathy, and letter dated March 27, 1933, from Monroe Abernathy to Judge Frost Woodhull, James W. Jarrott Reference File, and folder on Mollie Abernathy and Monroe Abernathy, Southwest Collections Library, Texas Tech University Lubbock, Texas; David J. Murrah, *Oil, Taxes and Cats: A History of the DeVitt Family and the Mallet Ranch* (Lubbock: Texas Tech University Press, 1994), 35-36; Max Coleman, "Who Killed This Man?" *Frontier Times* magazine, September 31, 1931.

5. Terry County Historical Survey Committee, *Early Settlers of Terry County: A History of Terry County, Texas* (Hereford, Texas: Pioneer Book Publishers, 1968), 11; Wingfield, "M. V. Brownfield's Colorful Career Is Recollected by Kin," *Terry County Herald*, December 3, 1937.

6. The Terry County [Texas] Historical Commission, *Terry County, Texas*, county history (private publisher, 2002), 230-231; H. Allen

Anderson, "Brownfield, Marion Virgil," *The New Handbook of Texas* (Austin: The Texas State Historical Association, 1996), 771-772; Handbook of Texas online, (http://www.txhaonline.org/handbook/online/articles/fbrdn).

7. *Terry County Herald*, December 3, 1937; *Terry County, Texas*, county history, 230-231.

8. Ibid.

9. Ibid.

10. Rick Miller, *Sam Bass and Gang* (Austin: State House Press, 1999), 64-67.

11. Ibid., 241-262.

12. *Terry County, Texas*, county history, 230-231.

13. Ibid.

14. Ibid.

15. Ibid., 50-51.

16. Ibid., 52.

17. Warranty Deed from Z. T. Joiner to D. J. Howard, dated January 17, 1902, recorded in Vol. 2, Pg. 198, *Terry County Deed Records*, conveying to Howard Sections 87, 101, 103, and 113, Block T, Dallas & Wichita Survey in Terry County. Consideration stated: $896 cash and assumption of five annual installment notes of $338 each plus interest.

18. *Terry County, Texas*, county history, 52, 59.

19. Ibid., 53, 231.

20. Dick Brownfield later described the ordeal undertaken by himself and his best horse, "Brown Jug," a horse that Dick recalled as being a real "laster." Dick and Brown Jug made the ninety-mile journey across the prairie from their Terry County ranch to Stanton in one day, but

it wasn't a "straight-line" journey to Stanton. Dick and Brown Jug had to "zigzag from one [playa lake] watering hole to another [playa lake] watering hole." Plus, to make the journey in one day, they had to start early and arrive late. And the pace for such a trip was "lope a while, trot a while, and walk a while." *Terry County, Texas*, county history, 52.

21. Warranty Deed dated January 17, 1902, from Z. T. Joiner to D. J. Howard, Vol. 2, Pg. 198, *Terry County Deed Records*, conveying to D. J. Howard Sections 87, 101, 103, and 113, Block T, Dallas and Wichita Survey, Terry County, Texas. Consideration: $896 cash and obligation to pay six $338 promissory notes from Howard to Joiner each coming due on each December 1 from 1902-1906.

22. Warranty Deed dated January 23, 1903, from D. J. Howard to J. B. Miller, Vol. 2, pg. 308, *Terry County Deed Records*, conveying same four sections to J. B. Miller. Consideration: Assignement by J. B. Miller to D. J. Howard of one promissory note in sum of $3,900, note dated January 1, 1903, and payable in full on March 31, 1903, 90 days after date; said note was executed by T. J. Coggin and made payable to J. B. Miller. Miller then assigned Coggin's $3,900 promissory note to Hoard as payment for Howard's four sections of land. The $3,900 promissory note was secured by a first lien on a large tract of land in East Texas. Note: The grantee, J. B. Miller did not assume any obligation to Howard to pay Coggin's $3,900 90-day note if Coggin defaulted on payment to Howard, and strangely enough, Howard did not even reserve a lien in his deed to Miller allowing Howard to recover title to his four sections in the event Coggin defaulted.

23. Warranty Deed dated January 30, 1903, from J. B. Miller to W. H. Fisher, Vol. 2 Pg. 402, *Terry County Deed Records*, conveying same four sections to Fisher. Consideration: $4,100 cash. Fisher assumes no obligation to pay off Coggin's $3,900 note to Howard in event that Coggin defaults.

24. Warranty Deed from W. H. Fisher to A. M. "Dick" Brownfield, dated March 7, 1903, recorded in Vol. 2, Pg. 410, *Terry County Deed Records*,

conveying to Brownfield those same four sections. Consideration: $800 cash. Again, the grantee (Dick Brownfield) assumed no obligation to guarantee payment of the $3,900 Coggin note (to Howard) in the event of a default by Coggin.

25. *Terry County, Texas*, county history, 53.

26. *State v. James B. Miller*, Cause No. 16, 869 in the 48th Judicial District Court of Tarrant County, Texas.

27. Ibid.

28. *Fort Worth Record*, May 5, 1906.

29. The criminal careers of both Tom Morrison and T. J. Coggin did not end with the lynching of Jim Miller in 1909. Far from it, their criminal careers accelerated into much more than merely being handy defense witnesses. They became partners in the business of murder. In fact, Morrison became well known among the criminal element in West Texas and New Mexico as an employment agent for hit men, and at the same time, he played the role of a go-between shield for anyone who wanted to terminate an enemy yet retain his anonymity. Morrison received the fee, hired the hit man, paid him the agreed fee when the assassination was successfully completed all without ever revealing the source of the money.

Their most sensational case was the 1917 assassination in El Paso of a New Mexico cattle baron named Thomas Lyons, the owner of a million-acre-plus ranch. That mystery remained unsolved until Lyons' widow posted a $10,000 reward for the arrest and conviction of the killer or killers of her husband. That lured a previously convicted felon and low-life named W. G. Clark of Abilene, Texas, to step forward and identify the killers. That resulted in murder indictments being returned against T. J. Coggin, his younger brother, Millard Coggin, and Felix R. Jones of Abilene and Fort Worth. This was not Felix Jones's first trip around the block by any means; he had killed other men, and he and Clark had partnered in other crimes.

Clark also implicated Morrison as a behind-the-scenes accessory to the Lyons assassination, but Morrison was not indicted. Whomever was the money-man behind the scene spared no expense in hiring the best lawyers for the three defendants (and perhaps some officials connected with the prosecution). The result was that the indictments against both the Coggin brothers were allowed to die on the vine and were later dismissed. Only Felix Jones stood trial. He was convicted by the jury and sentenced to twenty-five years in prison. However, after having served only nine years he was granted a pardon by Texas Governor Miriam "Ma" Ferguson, who was noted for her very, very lenient pardon policy. She granted Jones an unconditional pardon without citing any person or official who had petitioned for a pardon.

During the murder trial of Felix Jones, Clark took the stand and testified that Tom Morrison was involved in the plot to kill Thomas Lyons. Morrison then took the stand and vehemently denied all of Clark's accusations; denounced him as a liar. At one point Morrison became so enraged that he exploded:

"When I have trouble with somebody I don't go to no court, but make it a personal matter."

Then, expressing "keen hatred" for the turncoat Clark, he added this:

"I would like to have him [Clark] out on my ranch and feed him on prickly pears."

Jerry J. Lobdill, *The Last Train to El Paso: The Mysterious Unsolved Murder of a Cattle Baron* (Fort Worth: Cross Timbers Press, 2014) 1, 50, 107-113, 183-190, 209-211, 205-211; *El Paso Herald*, February 16, 1918.

30. Murrah, *Oil, Taxes, and Cats*, 35-36.

31. *State of Texas v. William Barrington*, Cause No. 69 in the 50th Judicial District Court of Lubbock County, Texas.

32. Murrah, *Oil, Taxes, and Cats*, supra, 35.

33. McNabb, *Ropes Remembers*, supra, 5-6.

34. Mrs. Roy Wingered, "M. V. Brownfield's Colorful Career Is Recollected," *Terry County Herald*, December 3, 1937.

35. Chuck Lanehart, "A History Mystery: Who Shot J. W. Jarrott?" *Voice for the Defense* magazine, supra, 26.

EPILOGUE

1. Lara Fergerson, "Why History Matters: A Story from West Texas," excerpt from a talk given on October 28, 2013, by Fergerson, a Professor of History at Longwood University, Farmville, Virginia, as printed in the *Quanah Tribune-Chief*, December 6, 2013.

2. Robert A. Calvert and Arnold De Leon, *The History of Texas* (Wheeling, Illinois: Harlan Davidson Inc., 1980), 177.

3. Ronnie and Sandra McNabb, *Ropes Remembers* (Ropesville, TX: Nunn Printing Co., 1974), 6.

4. Murrah, *Oil, Taxes, and Cats*, 35.

5. S. V. Connor, ed., "The West Is for Us: The Reminiscences of Mary A. Blankenship," *The Museum Journal* (Lubbock: West Texas Museum Association, 1958), Vol. 2, 43.

6. Ida Lee Cowan, "Early Days on the Plains," *The Lubbock Avalanche-Journal*, January 13, 1924.

7. J. Evetts Haley and William Curry Holden, *The Flamboyant Judge James J. Hamlin* (Canyon, TX: Palo Duro Press, 1972), 11-13.

8. Exley, *Texas Tears and Texas Sunshine*, 253.

9. Lawrence Lester Graves, "Wallace Blankenship," *Builders of the Southwest*, Seymour V. Connor, ed. (Lubbock: Southwest Collection, Texas Technological College, 1959), 22-25; John Hope, *Texas' Last Frontier*

Ranch Heritage Tour, 2011 Guide Book, Sponsored jointly by Hockley County and Cochran County, Texas Historical Commissions, 62.

10. Connor, "The West Is for Us," 43; Jo Ella Powell Exley, *Texas Tears and Texas Sunshine: Voices of Frontier Women* (College Station: Texas A&M University Press, 1985), 250.

11. Ray Sylvan Dunn, "A. W. and Mary Blankenship," *Builders of the Southwest*, 21.

12. Connor, "Mollie D. Abernathy," *Builders of the Southwest*, 5.

13. Murrah, *Oil, Taxes, and Cats*, 36-37.

14. Ibid., 223-224.

15. Ibid., 228-230.

16. Mollie and Monroe Abernathy, interview by Seymour V. Connor, 4 and 7 June 1956, tape recording, tape two, Southwest Collection, Texas Tech University, Lubbock, Texas.

17. Seymour V. Conner, "Abernathy, Mollie Wyley," *The New Handbook of Texas* (Austin: The Texas State Historical Association, 1996), 7; Handbook of Texas online (http://www.txhaonline.org/handbook/online/articles/flrdr).

Bibliography

BOOKS

Armitage, Shelley. *Walking the Llano: A Texas Memoir of Place.* Norman: University of Oklahoma Press, 2016.

Berry, Howard K. *He Made It Safe to Murder: The Life of Moman Pruiett.* Oklahoma City: Oklahoma Heritage Association, 2001.

Blassingame, Ike. *Dakota Cowboy: My Life in the Old Days.* New York: G. P. Putman's Sons, 1958.

Brasher, Lillian. *Hockley County, 1921-1971.* Canyon, TX: The Staked Plains Press, 19_ .

Calvert, Robert A. and De Leon Arnold. *The History of Texas.* Wheeling, IL: Harlan Davidson Inc., 1980.

Campbell, Ida Foster, and Alice Foster Hill. *Triumph and Tragedy: A History of Thomas Lyons and the L C.s.* Silver City, NM: High-Lonesome Books, 2002.

Campbell, Randolph B. *Gone to Texas: A History of the Lone Star State.* New York and Oxford: Oxford University Press, 2003.

Carlson, Paul H. *Amarillo: The Story of a Western Town.* Lubbock: Texas Tech University Press, 2006.

———. *Empire Builder in the Texas Panhandle: William Henry Bush.* College Station: Texas A&M University Press, 1996.

Conner, Seymour V., ed. *The West Is for Us: The Reminiscences of Mary A. Blankenship.* Lubbock: West Texas Museum Association, 1958.

Exley, Jo Ella. *Texas Tears and Texas Sunshine: Voices of Frontier Women.* College Station: Texas A&M University Press, 1985.

Fairchild, Louis. *The Lonesome Plains: Death and Revival on an American Frontier.* College Station: Texas A&M University Press, 2002.

Gardner, Mark Lee. *To Hell on a Fast Horse: Billy the Kid, Pat Garrett, and the Epic Chase to Justice in the Old West.* New York: Harper Collins Publishers, 2010.

Greene, A. C. *Sketches from the Five States of Texas.* College Station: Texas A&M University Press, 1998.

Haley, J. Evetts. *Charles Goodnight: Cowman and Plainsman.* Norman: University of Oklahoma Press, 1949.

———. *The XIT Ranch of Texas and the Early Days of Llano Estacado.* Norman: University of Oklahoma Press, 1967.

Haley, J. Evetts and William Curry Holden. *James D. Hamlin, The Flamboyant Judge: The Story of Amarillo and the Development of the Great Ranches of the Texas Panhandle.* Canyon: Palo Duro Press, 1972.

Harkey, Dee. *Mean as Hell: The Life of a New Mexico Lawman.* Santa Fe: Ancient City Press, 1989.

Hope, John. *Texas' Last Frontier Ranch Heritage Tour, 2011 Guide Book.* Sponsored jointly by Hockley County and Cochran County, Texas Historical Commissions.

James, Bill C. *Jim Miller: The Untold Story of a Texas Badman.* Wolfe City, TX: Henington Publishing Company, 1989.

Keleher, William A. *The Fabulous Frontier.* Santa Fe: The Rydal Press, 1942.

Knight, Sherri. *Vigilantes to Verdicts: Stories from a Texas District Court.* Stephenville: Jacobus Books, 2009.

Lobdill, Jerry. *Last Train to El Paso: The Mysterious Unsolved Murder of a Cattle Baron.* Fort Worth: Cross Timbers Press, 2014.

Marcy, Randolph B. *Captain U.S. Army. The Prairie Traveler.* Bedford, Me: Applewood Books, 1986 (originally published in 1859).

McNabb, Ronnie, and Shirley McNabb. *Ropes Remembers.* Ropesville, TX: Nunn Printing Co. 1974.

Metz, Leon C. *Pat Garrett: The Story of a Western Lawman.* Norman: University of Oklahoma Press, 1974.

Miller, Rick. *Sam Bass and Gang.* Austin: State House Press, 1999.

Moffat, Riley. *Population of Western U.S. Cities and Towns, 1850-1900.* Lanham, MD: Scarecrow Press, 1996.

Morris, John Miller. *El Llano Estacado: Exploration and Imagination on the High Plains of Texas and New Mexico, 1530-1860.* Austin: Texas State Historical Association, 1997.

Murrah, David. *Oil, Taxes, and Cats: A History of the DeVitt Family and the Mallet Ranch.* Lubbock: Texas Tech University Press, 1994.

———. *C. C. Slaughter: Rancher, Banker, Baptist.* Austin: University of Texas Press, 1981.

Neal, Bill. *From Guns to Gavels: How Justice Grew Up in the Outlaw West.* Lubbock: Texas Tech University Press, 2008.

———. *Vengeance Is Mine: The Scandalous Love Triangle That Triggered the Boyce-Sneed Feud.* Denton: University of North Texas Press, 2011.

Nordyke, Lewis. *Cattle Empire: The Fabulous Story of the 3,000,000 Acre XIT.* New York: William Morrow, 1949.

Parsons, Chuck, and Norman Brown. *A Lawless Breed: John Wesley Hardin, Texas Reconstruction, and Violence in the Wild West.* Denton: University of North Texas Press, 2013.

Perkins, Yvonne Spence, and Judy Womack. *Death on the Plains: The Murder of Jim Jarrott.* Private Printing, 2010, Southwest Collection Library, Texas Tech University, Lubbock, Texas.

Pruiett, Moman. *Criminal Lawyer.* Oklahoma City: Harlow Publishing Corp., 1944.

Richardson, Rupert N. *Texas: The Lone Star State.* New York: Prentice-Hall, 1943.

Shirley, Glenn. *Shotgun for Hire: The Story of "Deacon" Jim Miller.* Norman: University of Oklahoma Press, 1970.

Sonnichsen, C. L. *Texas Feuds: "Vengeance Is Mine!" Saith the Lord, But in Texas He Has Always had Plenty of Help!* Albuquerque: University of New Mexico Press, 1971.

Spivey, Broadus, and Jesse Sublett. *Broke Not Broken: Homer Maxey's Texas Bank War.* Lubbock: Texas Tech University Press, 2014.

Webb, Walter Prescott, *The Great Plains.* Lincoln: University of Nebraska Press, 1959 (originally published in New York: Gosset & Dunlap, 1931).

ARTICLES

Alvord, Wayne. "T. L. Nugent: Texas Populist." *Southwestern Historical Quarterly* Austin: Texas State Historical Commission, 1953.

Anderson, H. Allen. "Brownfield, Marion Virgil." *The New Handbook of Texas.* Austin: Texas Historical Association, 1996.

Archambeau, Ernest. "The Fort Smith-Santa Fe Trail Along the Canadian River in Texas." *Panhandle-Plains Historical Review*, Canyon, TX, 1954.

Billingsley, William C. "The Strip." *Recollections from the Heart of Hockley County.* Dallas: Taylor Publishing Company, 1986.

Brownfield, A. M. "Struggle for School Land: Purchasers Scramble for Number One Chair in Clerk's Office: Rivals Slip in by Night To Catch Guards Napping." *Terry County Herald*, December 17, 1937.

Burka, Paul. "The Open Range R.I.P., 1866-1884." *Texas Monthly* magazine, January 1986.

Carlson, Paul. "100 Years Ago on the Llano Estacado." *Llano Estacado Heritage*, Summer, 1975.

Coleman, Max. "Who Killed This Man?" *Frontier Times* magazine, September 1931.

Conner, Seymour V. "The West Is for Us: The Reminiscences of Mary Blankenship." Lubbock: *West Texas Museum Association Journal*, 1958.

———. "Mollie D. Abernathy." *Builders of the Southwest.* Lubbock: Southwest Collection, Texas Technological College, 1959.

———. "Mollie Wylie Abernathy." *The New Handbook of Texas.* Austin: Texas State Historical Association, 1996.

Cowan, Mrs. Ida Lee. "Early Days on the Plains." The *Lubbock Morning Avalanche*, June 13, 1924.

Dibrell, Jeanne. "Four-Sections Act." *The New Handbook of Texas*, Austin: Texas State Historical Association, 1996.

Dole, F. L. "The West Made Habitable by Windmills." *The Cattleman* magazine, No. 19, October 1932.

Dunn, Roy Sylvan. "A. W. and Mary Blankenship." *Builders of the Southwest*. Lubbock: Southwest Collection, Texas Technological College, 1959.

Fergeson, Lara. "Why History Matters: A Story from West Texas." *Quanah [Texas] Tribune-Chief*, December 6, 2013.

Gard, Wayne. "Fence Cutting," *The New Handbook of Texas*, Austin: Texas State Historical Association, 1996.

Graham, Don. "Notes from Texas." *On Writing in the Lone Star State*. Fort Worth: TCU Press, 2008.

Graves, Lawrence Lester. "Wallace Blankenship." *Builders of the Southwest*. Lubbock: Southwest Collection, Texas Technological College, 1959.

Holt, R. D. "School Land Rushes in West Texas." *The West Texas Historical Association Journal*, Abilene, 1934.

Hope, John. "Jim Jarrott and The Strip." *Texas' Last Frontier Ranch Heritage, 2010 Tour Guide Book*. Hockley and Cochran County Historical Commissions.

James, Edwin. "Account of an Expedition from Pittsburgh to the Rocky Mountains, Performed in the Years 1819 and 20...under the Command of Major Stephen H. Long." *Early Western Travels*, ed. R. G. Thwaites. Ohio: Arthur H. Clark, 1905.

Landis, Lawrence A. "Lanham, Samuel Willis Tucker." *The New Handbook of Texas*. Austin: Texas State Historical Commission, 1996.

Lanehart, Chuck. "A History Mystery: Who Shot J. W.?" *Voice for the Defense* magazine, May 2011.

Leatherwood, Art. "Llano Estacado," *The New Handbook of Texas.* Austin: Texas Historical Society, 1996.

Lindsey, Ellis. "Did Miller Kill Pat Garret?" *Wild West* magazine, October 2011.

Miller, Worth Robert. "Nugent, Thomas Lewis." *The New Handbook of Texas,* Austin: Texas State Historical Commission, 1996.

Rickards, J. A. "South Plains Land Rushes." *Panhandle-Plains Historical Review,* Canyon, TX, 1929.

Steele, June M. "Mollie Abernathy: Rancher of the South Plains, 1900-1909." *West Texas Historical Association Journal,* Lubbock, 1999.

Terry County Historical Commission. "Notorious Badman 'Deacon Jim Miller'." *Terry County, Texas.* Clanton, AL: Heritage Publishing Consultants, 2002.

Terry County Historical Survey Committee. "J. W. Jarrott." *Early Settlers of Terry: A History of Terry County, Texas.* Hereford, TX: Pioneer Book Publishers, 1968.

Todd IV, William N. "Rogan, Charles." *The New Handbook of Texas,* Austin: Texas State Historical Commission, 1996.

Turner, Leland. "The West Texas Plains." *West Texas: A History of the Giant Side of the State.* Norman: University of Oklahoma Press, 2014.

———. "Grassland, Beef Factories: Frontier Cattle Raisers in Northwest Texas and the Queensland Outback." *Panhandle-Plains Historical Review,* Canyon, TX, 2015.

Watkins, Orville R. "Hockley County: From Cattle Ranches to Farmers." *West Texas Historical Association Yearbook,* Abilene, 1941.

Wingered, Mrs. Roy. "M. V. Brownfield's Colorful Career Is Recollected." *Terry County Herald,* December 3, 1937.

INTERNET ARTICLES

Anderson, Allen. "Brownfield, Marion Virgil," The *New Handbook of Texas,* Austin: The Texas State Historical Association, 1996. *The New*

Handbook of Texas online, (http://www.txhaonline.org/handbook/online/articles/fbrdn)

THESES

Buchner, Kyle. "History of Terry County," Master's thesis, Texas Technological College, Lubbock, Texas, 1943.

Mitchell, Glen H. "Three Major Crises in the Life of Terry County," Master's thesis, Texas Technological College, Lubbock, Texas, 1957.

NEWSPAPERS

Ada Evening News

Shawnee Daily Herald

El Paso Herald

Fort Worth Star-Telegram

Fort Worth Morning Register

Fort Worth Record

Dallas Morning News

Lubbock Avalanche-Journal

Lubbock Morning Avalanche

Terry County Herald

The Galveston News

Quanah Tribune-Chief

LEGAL DOCUMENTS

LAWS

Gammel, Laws of State of Texas, (1895 as amended 1897), 10:63-77), General Laws of Texas, 793-807.

Gammell, comp. Laws of the State of Texas, 1822-1897; Vol. 10, H. B. No. 30, 25th Legislature (Austin: Gammel, 1898), 1480.

TRIAL COURT CASES

State v. J. B. Miller, Cause No. 16,869, Tarrant County, Texas, District Court.

State v. J. B. Miller, Cause No. 1,132, Eastland County, Texas, District Court.

State v. B. F. Nix, Cause No. 67, Lubbock County, Texas, District Court.

State v. B. F. Nix, Cause No. 68, Lubbock County, Texas, District Court.

State v. B. F. Nix, Cause No. 69, Lubbock County, Texas, District Court.

State v. William Barrington, Cause No. 69, Lubbock County, Texas, District Court.

State v. J. W. Barrington, Cause No. 70, Lubbock County, Texas, District Court.

State v. Morgan Bellow, Cause No. 71, Lubbock County, Texas, District Court.

State v. B. G. Glaser, Cause No. 71, Lubbock County, Texas, District Court.

APPELLATE COURT CASES

James B. Miller v. State of Texas, Cause No. 3283, 18 Tex.Ct.Crim.App. 232, May 20, 1885.

Ketner v. Rogan, et al., 95 Tex. 559, 68 S.W. 774 Tex. Sup. Ct., 1902.

Miller v. State of Texas, 43 Tex.Ct.Crim.App. 367; 65 S.W. 908, 1901.

RECORDS

Warranty Deed: dated January 17, 1902 [1903?], from Z. T. Joiner to D. J. Howard, Vol. 2, Pg. 198, Terry County Deed Records, conveying to D. J. Howard Sections 87, 101, 103, and 113, Block T, Dallas and Wichita Survey, Terry County, Texas. Consideration: $896 cash plus six promissory notes totaling $2,088. Deed was notarized by J. B. Miller.

Warranty Deed: dated January 23, 1903, from D. J. Howard to J. B. Miller. Vol. 2, Pg. 308, Terry County Deed Records, conveying same four sections to J. B. Miller. Consideration: assignment by J. B. Miller to D. J. Howard of one promissory note in sum of $3,900, note dated January 1, 1903, and payable in full ninety days after date (March 31, 1903); said note was executed by T. J. Coggin and made payable to J. B. Miller. Grantor D. J. Howard fails to reserve any lien on his land in event of default by T. J. Coggin in paying his $3,900 note.

Warranty Deed dated January 30, 1903, from J. B. Miller to W. H. Fisher, Vol. 2 Pg. 402, Terry County Deed Records, conveying same four sections to Fisher. Consideration (at least according to the deed recital) $4,100.

Warranty Deed dated March 7, 1903, from W. H. Fisher to A. M. "Dick" Brownfield, recorded in Vol. 2, Pg. 410 conveying same four sections to Brownfield. Consideration: $800.

PRIVATE LETTERS OF RECORD

Randolph B. Marcy, letter to the Secretary of War George W. Crawford, Feb. 21, 1850, "Route from Fort Smith to Santa Fe," H. Exec. Doc. 45, 31st Cong., 1st Session, p. 41.

Letter dated March 23, 1933, from Jack Abernathy to M. G. Abernathy, James W. Jarrott Reference file, Southwest Collections Library, Texas Tech University, Lubbock, Texas.

Letter dated March 27, 1933, from Monroe Abernathy to Judge Frost Woohull, James W. Jarrott Reference File, Southwest Collections Library, Texas Tech University, Lubbock, Texas.

ORAL RECORDS (INTERVIEWS)

Conner, Seymour V. Tape One of tape-recorded interview of Mollie and Monroe Abernathy, June 4 and 7, 1956, Southwest Collection, Texas Tech University, Lubbock, Texas.

Cowan, Lee. [Terry County, Texas] *Pioneers and Primrose School.* Interview notes in possession of John and Bette Hope, Levelland, Texas.

Daniels, Anna Laura Cowan. [Memoirs of Her Father], *Lee Cowan, Early Terry County, Texas, Settler.* Interview notes in possession of John and Bette Hope, Levelland, Texas.

Nunn Sr., James H. interview by Omah Ryan, 1937, pp. 3-5, Research Center, Panhandle-Plains Museum, Canyon, Texas.

REPORTS

Personnel File of the Texas State Government with Sketches of Distinguished Texans, Embracing The Executive and Staff, Heads of the Departments, United States Senators and Representatives, Members of the Twentieth Legislature, Compiled and Published by L. E. Daniel, (Austin: Press of the City Print Company, 1887), J. W. Jarrott, p. 142.

May 17, 1902, Report of [Texas] State Legislative Investigating Committee, pages 113-115; Google Books, *http:/books.google.com/books?id.* Investigation of complaints of South Plains ranchers, and Lubbock County officials accusing Texas General Land Office Commissioner, Charles Rogan, of favoritism in awarding the Four-Sections Act claims of J. W. Jarrott and eight of his settlers clients on April 24, 1902. Commissioner Rogan overruled complaints and the Investigating Committee upheld Rogan's decision.

Index

LYNDHURST PUBLIC LIBRARY, NJ
3 9106 09162705 9